THE POWER OF OH

Adam Bourgeois

THE POWER OF OH

A Path to Growth, Insight, Appreciation of Self and Others

Cover Illustration (Picture Card 67)

Text Illustrations (Picture Cards 1-88, incl.)

Eos Interactive Cards **www.OH-Cards.com**

Impressum

Chicago, Illinois

Printed in Germany

Layout: G. Bruckmann, Trier

ISBN 1-896018-46-7

TO THE MEMORY OF MELLONIE

Her Dreams Continue to Teach Us.

ACKNOWLEDGMENTS

It is with gratitude that I acknowledge the many persons who have had an impact upon my thinking over the years in my pursuit of the mysteries of life.

They are the writers, teachers, and students who have shared their wisdom and family and friends who have shared their encouragement and love.

Each has been significant to my life experience: Mary Lou Bourgeois, Prescott A. Bourgeois, and Yvonne Schubert; Iona Hubbard and Ben Hubbard; Walter Bourgeois; Horace Lomax; Charley Kimmel; Sister Alma, S.B.S., Sister Laetitia, S.B.S., and Sister "Bill," S.B.S.; Allen Lenard and Marlenė Lenard; Gil Segal and Joanne Segal; Dick Gregory; Eileen Poole; Katrina Kessler and Poppy; Selma Sachs; Luella Overeem; Connie Simons; George Philosophos; Karyn Safron; Pamela Wolf; Mellonie Hubert; Kimberley Robinson; Dave Rice, Therese Cesar; Bettie Smiley, Ruth Liss; Barbara Biziou; Grace J. Van Atta; Wilma Van Atta; Bert Lassche; Mo Egetmeyer; Ely Raman; Florence Shinn; Joel Goldsmith; Marie-Louise von Franz; Carl Jung; Naju; and Dr. Brugh Joy.

Each has been a blessing but none more than my wife, Barbara Klein.

Adam Bourgeois

CONTENTS

INTRODUCTION

This book by Adam Bourgeois is a journey led by a very able guide into the realm of the soul, the realm of the psyche: The place from which all essential waters of life flow. And like all good guides, Adam tells us of his experiences with appropriate respect for our own journey. His is not the voice of the expert who tells us what to see, what to do, or think, or imagine.

Adam's is the voice of the experienced traveler sharing the delights of his adventures, pointing out exotic corners and wondrous vistas. We are urged to explore further on our own and to find our own delights.

These are the comments of Ely Raman, the artist, co-author of *The Little Book About The OH Cards,* and inventor of the OH Cards, which are the subject matter of this book. In his opening chapter, Adam sets forth his purpose and he refers to Moses' urging to "choose life" and to Joseph Campbell's counsel to "catch life." Adam says that the OH Cards are a tool to use to go beyond the ordinary and to step into the extraordinary world of self-knowledge. The OH Cards make self-explorers of people.

OH Cards are fitted for such use because they are adaptable to different ethnic backgrounds and cultural traditions and are flexible for many different personal or professional purposes by a single individual or a group. There are 176 cards in OH and they are divided into two decks: One of 88 different paintings and the other of 88 different words. Together the two decks symbolize the counterparts of rationality (words) and of intuition (images) and are a pathway to the synthesis of the two.

The cards reflect Ely Raman's investigation of "variable structures" in art and of avant-garde influences, including those of Marcel Duchamp and John Cage. The fact that art is usually viewable only in galleries or is performed on a stage fosters the belief in people that the creative process lies outside of themselves. The notion is that "They are creative and I am not." Ely transforms this through the vehicle of the OH Cards.

The OH Cards have become Ely's best known and most widely published variable structure; they are the realization of his goal of putting art into the hands of the viewer and including the viewer in the creative process. Unlike an inert painting hanging on a museum wall, OH Cards are designed to be interactive and are meant to be touched. In the process of working with the OH Cards, users bring their personal intuition and individual experience to bear in order to complete the meaning the cards have for them.

When cards are selected at random and are complemented with personal perceptions and associations, the cards spring to life. Their 7,744 word and image combinations lead to an infinite number of meanings when they are touched by personal interpretations. The cards were given the name "OH" – the most common word in English to express surprise – because they so often reveal the unexpected.

The OH Cards consistently demonstrate their worth to me by the many examples of how people have used them. For instance, an Israeli, who is a university professor and trauma therapist, is on call to go to the locations of major disasters. In the aftermath of a devastating earthquake in Turkey, she used the OH Cards as a device in training psychologists who were there to help victims cope with loss of loved ones, their homes, and their livelihoods and to help rescue workers deal with the stress of their overwhelming task.

In Finland, social workers at shelters for mothers and children use the OH Cards to help them tell their inner stories. In Holland, storytellers take them into schools. A center for creative writing in Munich and team-trainers for an automobile producer in a nearby city both use OH Cards to open channels to their intuition and creativity. The OH Cards are used in psychodrama groups in England, by kinesiologists in New Zealand, and by dance teachers and fashion designers in New York. With OH in print in 15 languages, there are thousands of people using the OH Cards all over the world.

Over the years the OH Cards have become an internationally recognized tool for both personal and interpersonal exploration. The unique strength of OH is that users become their own best authorities and do not need to rely on prescribed solutions. This is no small feat, considering the human temptation of most persons to lead or be led. In my estimation, the mark of a great tool is that it can be used in many meaningful and creative ways. Like a box of paints or a musical instrument, playing the OH Cards is a hands-on experience and is a means to find answers and to reach the resources which exist within all people.

In this book, Adam brings the considerable power of his intelligence and erudition to bear on the OH Cards and in the chapters which follow demonstrates the potential of the OH Cards to explore the realms of the psyche as the path to self-knowledge. Adam has worked with the OH Cards for many years and he has also introduced them to friends and associates and organized study groups around the OH Cards.

In his groups, Adam has worked with hundreds of people, who have extended the OH Cards beyond the group and into their own realms. An example is a woman in Adam's group who is using the OH Cards for her doctoral thesis research. A notable personal experience of hers is included in Chapter 4 in which she has described a "whirlwind of psychic energy" she encountered after use of the OH Cards. The book is filled with many interesting examples and provocative illustrations of the OH Cards in use.

The book is organized into three parts. In Part I of his book, Adam discusses the OH Cards and the realms of personal discovery – the conscious, the unconscious, and archetypes. These chapters prepare the way for Part II and Part III which are about the 176 OH Cards and his insights and comments on each individual card, drawing upon myth, fairytales, word histories, and universal symbols.

W. Brugh Joy, M.D., author of *Joy's Way - A Map of the Transformational Journey*, commented about Adam's book: "The OH Cards are a wondrously useful, intuitive tool to access the forces that lie behind an event or question. In Adam Bourgeois' hands the two decks of OH, one each of words and pictures, become both oracular and revelatory. He delves into the symbolism of the cards and shows how they trigger emotions, intuitions, feelings, fantasies, and ideas to express our innermost realms."

Dick Gregory, political and social commentator and activist, entertainer, writer, and author of *Callus On My Soul*, said: "Adam Bourgeois and I discovered the world of the metaphysical together many years ago. We have explored the inner workings of the psyche in cities around the world, Paris, Montreal, Moscow, Athens, Rome, London, Puerto Vallarta, Casablanca, Cairo, as well as throughout the United States. During this time, Adam has honed his skills as a reader and a teacher. He takes calls from all over at all hours. In this book he passes on some of his wonderful philosophy and knowledge. He gave me a set of OH Cards when he first found them, and for us OH has proved to be the best personal tool for self-development that I know of. This magnificent book will do the same for its readers."

Barbara Biziou, author of *The Joy of Ritual* and *The Joy of Family Rituals*, also commented: "Adam illustrates the ease with which you can use the OH Cards to explore your deepest secrets and the joy that comes with the rewards of understanding. He is a true teacher and guide. Don't miss a chance to learn from him."

Adam has made a unique and workable tool of the cards for himself and has guided other people in their efforts to do the same. Through this book he shares with a yet wider public his knowledge and experience. Since the meaning of an OH Card is always individual and subjective and relative to the moment of the question, Adam offers his observations and comments for the reader to use as a workbook to expand and build upon for self-activation.

Moritz Egetmeyer, Publisher

Eos Interactive Cards

PART I

KNOW THYSELF

The inscription on the oracle of Apollo at Delphi

This is the generation of 24/7, a term of reference making its way into the vocabulary which means that you can get hold of just about anybody in any place 24 hours a day, seven days a week. People everywhere are caught up with being connected. It is like what happens at sports events across the globe when a movement of people in a large crowd, acting like a wave, successively rise, lift their arms overhead, and quickly sit, all catching the exhilaration of the swell moving through the crowd.

There are multiple means and gadgets to meet the endless quest to get through faster and better not only for business but also for personal use. Messages travel on wire or wireless, by analog or digital technology. They race at lightning speed along cable or bounce by microwave from tower to tower or by satellite link to connect across the country or across town. Voice mail, call waiting, three-way calling, call forwarding, faxing, paging, and e-mail are means widely employed. Contact can be made from an automobile on the highway or an airplane in flight.

The internet provides another dimension to being in touch. It is said that 250,000,000 individuals are on the internet with seven new users coming on line every second. Internet chat rooms are filled with people interacting in casual banter or in a serious effort to cultivate cyberspace relationships. When persons are unable to Reach Out and Touch Someone®, as the advertisement goes, they turn to other sources. They listen in by the millions to talk radio, including callers from halfway around the world tuned in on the internet. Television is also a compelling medium: Both the saga of President Clinton and the trial of O. J. Simpson kept a large segment of the populace of the United States enthralled for over a solid year. The search is for intimacy whether the contact is impersonal and anonymous or through ersatz relationships with personalities in the news headlines.

The urge to be in touch 24 hours a day, seven days a week, is more than a compulsion for socialization. This activity and the technological and marketing accoutrements are the expression of a deeper primal human impulse. It is a symptomatic manifestation of an inner state of the individual which is the push of the unconscious to be in touch with the conscious – to avail the psyche of its totality. To connect is the instinctual response in human nature to bridge the schism between the unconscious and the conscious and to link these dual realities. As long as the focus remains exclusively outward, it is misdirected. Inevitably, the search must couple the outer reality of the visible world of the conscious with the inner reality of the invisible world of the unconscious.

Instead of concentrating only on what is going on in the world outside, turning within opens the door to living a balanced existence. Religion, geography, education, ethnic background, family, and other cultural influences by their very nature limit consciousness. Such constraints hold no sway over the unconscious. The unconscious is a source without limits containing not only personal memories but also the memories of all cultures which have ever existed. It is a virtual bottomless pit of encyclopedic knowledge at our disposal.

Joseph Campbell spoke about this in *The Power of Myth*, commenting that individuals are so busy with things that hold outer value for themselves that the inner value is overlooked. Moses instructs the Israelites to "choose life" (*Deuteronomy* 30:19). Campbell would add that we should also work to "catch life" – the rapture of being alive. The purpose of this book is to introduce the OH Cards as a tool for the person who is seeking to go beyond the ordinary and step into the extraordinary world of self-knowledge. Through words and images, OH becomes a wise adviser and a considerate friend.

MEETING OH FOR THE FIRST TIME

Chances are that the reader of this book has a set of the OH Cards and may already be using them or is someone who is about to take the cellophane wrap from a box to try them out for the first time.

Whatever the circumstance may be – whether a person is an old hand or using the cards for the first time – the key ingredient in using the OH Cards is the imagination.

Lying dormant, the OH Cards are paper stock and ink. In use, the cards become an extension of both the conscious and the unconscious. The cards are a universe of symbols expressed in colors, numbers, abstract and concrete images, in spirit, and in words. The OH Cards as symbolic art are by their very nature ideally suited for self-examination and personal inquiry.

OH is a set of two decks of cards, one deck of picture cards and one deck of word cards. The deck of picture cards has a different painting on each card. The deck of word cards, which is slightly larger, has a different word on each card and the word is repeated on each border of the card.

The subject matter of the picture and word cards calls to mind the experiences of life. The images are contemporary in nature and may suggest something simple or complex, animate or inanimate, abstract or concrete, obvious or ambiguous. Examples of the depictions on the picture cards are men, women, and children, plants and animals, landscapes, still lifes, exterior and interior scenes. The card renderings are wide-ranging and not in any particular order.

Ely Raman, who created the original picture cards as watercolor paintings, feels very strongly about reawakening people to their innate capacities and creativity. Ely believes that offering art in the form of playing cards demystifies art – it takes it out of the museums and galleries – and brings it back to the imaginative response of each individual.

Initially Ely used only picture cards, but like pictures, words also evoke many meanings and were added as a further stimulus and provocation to the imagination. All art derives from the right brain, the section of the brain from which come dreams. OH sprang from the unconscious of their creator, Ely Raman. The words were his conscious choices.

The OH Cards can be used by one person for self-exploration or with several persons to exchange feelings, ideas, and intuitions. Suggested uses are to play games of story-telling and invention; to stimulate creativity, imagination, and fantasy; to enhance communication and encourage expression; and to build self-awareness.

The printed literature enclosed with the cards stresses that the OH cards are designed for free-association, free-wheeling interpretation, and a willingness to indulge the imagination. "An OH exploration is like a poem. Images arise that at first glance seem out of context, but on closer examination open new vistas of meaning," Ely has said.

The drawings are open-ended and foster many interpretations. The same is true of the word cards. Generally the two decks are used together: A card is pulled from each deck with the picture card placed on top of the word card. Players of the OH Cards are entirely responsible for what they are seeing in a combination of cards; the OH Cards are free of any particular moral or conceptual system.

The publisher of the cards, Moritz Egetmeyer, and Ely concur that the OH Cards allow for "dynamic and undogmatic personal development." They suggest that no matter how they are used the purpose is always the same – to increase intuition and to provide insights. Through their use is gained insight into everyday activities, personal problems, and perplexing quandaries. The cards are available in 15 languages, attesting to the fact that they have universal appeal.

The OH Cards were introduced to me over ten years ago. I was attending a gathering at a friend's home and had been doing readings using a system I devised in which I interpret random numbers given to me by the seeker. When I started to do a reading for one of the guests, she pulled out her OH Cards. She had wrapped each deck in a silk cloth. She uncovered them and told me to take a card at random from each deck and to place the picture card on the word card. Then she told me to read what the cards say by using the first person – in stating my thoughts about the cards, to begin the sentence with "I . . . ." The first two cards I chose were an eyepopper for me: The picture card I pulled was a drawing of a calendar and a wrist watch (3). The word card I drew was FASCINATION (119).

The picture card reflected to me exactly what I had been doing at the time (the wristwatch on the card is a *time*piece). I use the date of birth when I use numbers – the picture card is of the dates on a calendar. Numbers have long held fascination for me. The word card was FASCINATION (119). The next day I immediately went looking for a set of OH Cards for my own. I have been using them in all sorts of situations for myself and with others ever since. Their flexibility is of great advantage and they foster open interaction whether used alone or in groups.

I had a Grandfather named Ben. He never had to avoid a phone call or a knock on the door because he said he never owed anything to anybody. His word was his bond, he was fond of saying. He worked on his father´s Mississippi farm behind a mule until he was 22 and probably would have stayed there much longer except that one evening his father chastised him and slapped him. He did not strike back. His father had always hit him when correcting or chastising Ben. His father was being the person he had always been. Now Ben realized a transition point had been reached and it was time to go. The knowlege he received was like a gift, a realization from within. He had an cpiphany at that moment and the realization that he was now a man, no longer a child. Without rancor or anger he left home the next day and traveled to Chicago where he lived the rest of his days.

At Christmas time every year Papa Ben would go out and purchase a very expensive bottle of bourbon, something he could not ordinarily afford. He would wrap it with colorful red and green paper and tie it with a bow. Every Christmas morning my mother announced the gifts. Eventually she would reach Ben´s gaily decorated box. As she said the name of who was receiving this gift and the name of who sent it, everyone, adult and child alike, would burst into laughter for the gift card always said: TO BEN, FROM BEN.

Use of the OH Cards has been very much like that for me. OH is a gift and is always one to myself from myself - To Adam, From Adam.

What has particularly struck me about the OH Cards as I have used them is their unique value as a collection of picture and word symbols. Each deck of the set contains 88 cards, a double 8 like a double spiral suggesting the two nucleotide coiling strands of DNA and fittingly the symbol of infinity. Through the imagery of their pictures and words, the OH Cards are a tool to express my inner world. With them I am mixing the unconscious messages and directives of the unconscious with my conscious world and the imaging faculty of imagination.

It is a fact that most seekers are unfamiliar with what symbols have come to represent. Less emphasis in today's society is placed on education in the classics and as a result fewer persons are conversant with mythology and philosophy or with the etymology of words or the origins of idiomatic expressions and phrases. The purpose of this writing is to include different perspectives in order to showcase the rich symbolism inherent within both the picture cards and word cards.

Included in this book are suggestions for interpreting each of the 176 cards of the two decks in terms of the universal symbolism of the cards. They can be found in the last two parts of the book. Picture cards are from 1 to 88. Word cards are from 89 to 176. Also included are two blank, unnumbered cards.

The descriptions of the pictures and the words represent personal insights, impressions, and intuitions concerning the symbolic meanings of the cards – how " I" see them. These are my intuitions and perceptions expressed in terms of the traditional symbols they suggest. There is much more that can be said about the cards than what I have written because in each new encounter with the cards there are added insights and understandings.

Ely Raman has expressed his wish that this book will serve "as a reference to stimulate others in their interaction with the actual cards." This expresses my purpose as well. Demonstrations of the cards in use will follow in subsequent chapters including my commentary on each of the picture and word cards. As I finish this introduction I turn to the OH Cards for comment and draw two cards. The cards were Word Card 25 and Picture Card 44. The message of these cards was a very clear confirmation of my desire and decision to write this book. The picture card was of a traffic signal with the green Go lighted up. The word card was GO.

BRINGING OH TO LIFE

At the outset of writing this commentary on the OH Cards, it occurred to me that I should demonstrate an actual and practical usage of the OH Cards. I started with OH itself for my first question. I asked OH to reveal to me its spiritual genesis, its function in the world of the unconscious. My second question was about this book: I asked OH to reveal to me insight into the writing itself. A third question was for a demonstration of the world of OH.

What OH revealed about its spiritual genesis: I took out my decks and from the picture cards I drew the Sun (39) and from the word cards SHARE (157).

The first work of the creator in all creation myths is the separation of light and darkness. Light always follows darkness in the order of cosmic development. Whether the story being told is that of the angel bringing the message to Abram or the dove bringing the Holy Spirit to Mary, or the story of the creation of the universe, it is a revelation of the power of light.

In terms of my interpretation of the cards I drew, this is how OH defines itself: Use of the cards is light shed upon my life, a guide for me to generate self-knowledge and to gain self-understanding. Classically, the Sun brings light, form, and order out of chaos and darkness. The Sun brings the unconscious to light and shares itself for my conscious understanding. Through imagery – symbols and words – OH is the illuminator of my book of life.

What OH revealed about this writing: For my question about insight into writing about the OH Cards, once more I drew two more cards at random, one from each deck. The picture card was of a clown (88) and the word card was JOY (137)

The clown is among the most mysterious of all symbols. The clown almost always has a smiling countenance, looks playful, and appears ready to entertain. The clown seems oblivious and unperturbed by the misfortunes it endures. Its countenance and behavior are a masquerade because the clown pulls tricks and puts me on the defensive. I am wary when I see the clown and I dismiss the figure as not to be heeded or taken seriously.

The goofy costume and silly antics of the clown belie its true character and are meant to redirect my attention from the secrets which the clown conceals and cannot disclose. What is essential about the clown is not the outer appearance but that which is deeply hidden.

The clown expresses my purpose to use the symbols of the OH Cards to penetrate outward appearances in order to unravel hidden mysteries, the *anima* in men and the *animus* in women. The outer appearance of the clown is the *persona*. That which is deeply hidden is the anima/animus.

JOY expresses the spirit and accord of these writings with the OH Cards. The message is "Fear not: for, behold, I bring you good tidings of great joy, which shall be to all people." (*Luke* 2:10)

Following are my descriptions about each of the four cards which are from the comments in the final two sections of the book. I explore the cards individually in terms of the traditional symbols suggested by their pictures and words. Using the cards in an actual reading in a real life setting gives greater dimension to the meaning which has significance for me. My comments about the symbols are for means of stimulating the psyche where rationality, cause, and effect do not exist.

Picture Card 39. *Tribes which have survived from ancient times, like Aborigines, Pygmies, and Bushmen, look upon the Sun as the Eye of God. It is God's good eye. The Moon is God's evil eye. Our Sun provides light, heat, and life. On the other hand the Sun can bring about drought, even floods. Yet there are billions of suns in the heavens, stars constantly being born, burning brightly for eons and then dying. Our Sun is no different. One day it will die as well and our light, heat, and life will disappear. The Moon has no light of its own. It merely reflects the light of the Sun. Its symbol reflects dependence, the female principle, and periodic change. These are the symbols of the rhythms of life, from birth to death.*

• *Applying numerology, the Sun is One and the Moon is Two. It is notable that light always follows darkness in the order of cosmic development. Light and darkness are the first cosmic duality. It is the yin and yang. Just as yin always contains traces of yang and yang always has traces of yin, so too do light and darkness always have traces of each other. Because the Sun has such a dramatic impact on our lives, many solar rituals sprang up in early civilizations. Daily human sacrifices were made to the Sun. The blood of the victims was needed to feed the Sun. Sun worship produced civilizations of fear.*

• *Given this history of its symbolism, what does the Sun signify to me in this card? First, it signifies the Power of Light, the revelation I receive when I commune with my own dark side. When my unconscious unfolds and I acknowledge and embrace the buried part of my psyche, I am re-created. All secret societies have initiation rites which symbolize light coming into the life of the initiated and creating a new person. Second, the card signifies the bringing of order out of chaos, things in my life straightening themselves out; decadence becoming spirituality; disintegration becoming unity. Finally, the card symbolizes the creative spark which I carry with me always. All Egyptian mummies had an amulet symbolizing the Sun. This spark is with you no matter where you are or what your condition might be. In John 1:9, Jesus says, "I am the Light of the World." I am the Light of my world. I have no limitation except that which I impose upon myself.*

SHARE (Word Card 157). *I am dealing with that which I have coming or with that which I must give to another. The prize will be cut into shares. My percent has to do with who I am and when I first came to the scene. A lion's share is all there is. If I am the leader, I will mete out to others first. If I come late, I do not demand a regular share.*

• *Being around people, even in a crowded environment, stimulates the person who likes to share. The Sacred Arts are Healing, Dream Interpretation, Oracular Use, and Storytelling. Each of these is a form of sharing. To share is a form of participation in the divine. When I share the solution to a problem or when I learn through trial and error, I am sharing, even though the sharing is sometimes with me alone.*

Picture Card 88. *The clown is the reverse image of a king and thus has come to be the symbol of the king who has been murdered. A king speaks in a proper way, stands and walks in an auspicious way. A clown acts in the exact opposite manner. A clown is irreverent. A king is majestic. A clown does not recognize authority. A king is the authority. People are in awe of the king. A clown is in awe of nothing. Laughter is the clown's awe. A king has royal ceremonies. A clown ridicules everything sacred. To draw this card means that I am not taking things very seriously. I am relegating my inner king to a backseat while my less formal self holds sway.*

• *The grotesque make-up of the clown is meant to reflect his coarse interior. Do I truly reflect my inner self?*

• *The clown has a manner which causes us not to take things so seriously, especially ourselves. Laughter is the best medicine for all ills plus it is the most subtle way to overcome reality.*

JOY (Word Card 137). *Joy is an emotion of pure pleasure and supreme well-being. Ecstasy is a momentary sensation which lasts forever. I will never forget a moment of ecstasy and all during my life I recall it to experience more joy. Learning gaiety is an art. If I go around filled with worry, I do not find delight in everyday pleasures. The night should not fall before I have a treat in order to engender joy. Joy is a very necessary ingredient in my life and easy to come by in a smile or dish of chocolate ice cream.*

What OH revealed about its realm: Picture Card 67 was the image card I drew. The word card was blank.

The word card represented the unconscious, an unknown realm of my being where there are no words, only images.

The figures depicted on the picture card appear to be a female and a male, which I interpret as the archetypes of the anima/animus – which is a symbolic expression such as the OH Cards will generate. Their dance is symbolic of the interplay between the conscious and the unconscious.

As the OH Cards are used in a dynamic setting, they take on meanings related to the question or matter under concern and to the person at the center of the inquiry.

There may be carry-over from previous inquiries or entirely new revelations may unfold and they may be completely opposite to previous interpretations of cards that were drawn or perhaps even to the reappearance of the same card or combination of two cards.

The possibilities of the picture and word cards to explain, elucidate, and clarify are inexhaustible.

THE TWO PHENOMENA OF OH

It is useful to know about two phenomena when using the OH Cards. The first is the invariability of the subject matter of the inquiries. The second is the range of emotions which will surface.

The first phenomenon: *Identifiable Categories of Life.* When you reach for the OH Cards, the underlying reason for using the OH Cards in an inquiry will fall into identifiable categories. Themes will have to do with values and desires which repeat throughout the human life experience — Procreation, Sustenance, Eluding Discomfort, Order, Power, Status, Inquisitiveness, Vengeance, Physical Condition, Justice, Community, Independence, Survival, Honor, and Family.

Additional categories will be created out of these 15 subject matter areas where two or more categories are in play at the same time or are in conflict. They will always involve only the categories just listed. The brief comments which follow are made within the context of the OH Cards.

These are the basic desires and values in the lives of all people. They form the storyline in all novels, histories, poems, conversations, myths, and particularly in all dreams. These categories are the significant concerns of life.

PROCREATION. It should be no surprise that sex is a frequent focus of an inquiry. In the heyday of my childhood experiences with a Ouija® Board, I used to invite children my own age from about eight to twelve to sessions and the most frequent questions were always allusions to sex. Susie wanted to know whether Baby Charlie liked her. Harold was interested in Darlene and on and on. Years later after converting to Judaism I ran a booth at a Purim party where I wore a wizard's costume and gave readings. I used to try to change the subject, but I was never successful and stopped trying. Sex is a popular concern no matter what the age.

SUSTENANCE. The subject of food is broader than that which you chew and swallow. It has to do with every true appetite. A true appetite is one which satisfies a bodily or spiritual urge and promotes wholeness. False appetites satisfy passions. True appetites promote growth.

ELUDING DISCOMFORT. The questions concerning eluding discomfort revolve around a person's physical well-being. Remember that things do not hurt until you become frightened of them. Fear of the consequences of a disease or an injury always stirs pain.

ORDER. Order is sought by those whose lives are reflecting chaos.

STATUS. Prestige is a legitimate goal of human experience. Often persons who search for and find distinction are instruments for communal development.

POWER. The desire for power is the drive which propels those who become leaders. We live in a world where hierarchal dominance is a given. Power vests in the leader of the hierarchy throughout the animal world. It is the determinant of which rooster or chicken gets to peck first; which wolf leads the pack and gains the privileges of the alpha male and in the case of the alpha female bears the young; or which gorilla heads the pack and has the choice of the females. The same principle is at play with human beings. We gather in cults around the one with charisma, or the one with the wisdom, or the one with the magic voice. Primitive human beings with this exact same urge to be a part of a hierarchal structure had leaders just as we do. When primitive people encountered mystery, things they could not understand or phenomena they could not master, they created gods to explain these things, gods to protect them and gods to advise them. All religions were formed around this theme of power residing outside of ourselves.

INQUISITIVENESS. Maintaining interest is the seed of invention and exploration.

VENGEANCE. Vengeance comes in two forms, active and inactive. Active vengeance seeks an eye for an eye, while inactive vengeance simply lives well and turns the other cheek.

PHYSICAL CONDITION. Flow is health; congestion is not. We put a very high premium on body movement. Whether at work or at play, the body gets a full measure of exercise. We disdain bodies which become couch potatoes. We applaud athleticism. Exercise is one of our principal values.

JUSTICE. Justice means the leveling of the playing-field. Handouts are not relished except to make sure there is a floor beneath which no one will fall. Justice is the process whereby one receives one's due.

COMMUNITY. Community has to do with the human necessity of being involved with others. We exist in relationships and in groups. Rare is the person who has no such need and yet remains in a balanced state.

INDEPENDENCE. Independence is not the same as unrestrained license. A license confers the sanction to do certain things such as driving a car or flying a plane. Within independence is freedom and the encompassing duty to act responsibly toward oneself and others.

SURVIVAL. Survival reminds you that the price of deviance will be rejection in relationships or in the group. The role of scapegoat exists in every group and is a role which everyone seeks to avoid.

HONOR. Honor relates to those things in which you glory, that which makes you proud, whether for the hero in the battle or for keeping your lawn free of trash.

FAMILY. Family concerns the universal trait of loving and protecting those who fall within our immediate or extended family group. It begins with genetic relationships and grows to include everyone we love.

The second phenomenon: *Five Basic Emotions.* As the cards are turned over for viewing, they will trigger unconscious energies and arouse unexpected emotions. The emotion which is involved in consultation with the OH Cards is the second phenomenon relative to using them. The emotion may be a powerful shock, disbelief, or denial. Or, it may be delight and the response will be joy and laughter. The cards may awaken a long buried memory. Remembrance of a prior trauma or loss may evoke tears and despair. Or, there may be a healing of an emotional wound and there will be a release from long-held anger.

Anger, Disgust, Fear, Pleasure, and Surprise are the five basic emotions which will be experienced in varying intensity and which will manifest physiologically in respiration rate, change in blood pressure, increase in pulse rate, disturbance in digestion, perspiration, and the like. Following are examples of the five emotions and how that they may manifest with word cards and picture cards.

Examples of the OH Cards and the Emotions of ANGER, DISGUST, FEAR, PLEASURE, AND SURPRISE

The emotion of anger: For example, if I were to draw the word cards LIE, RIVAL, THREAT, COMPULSION, FAIL, ANGER, ATTACK or HATE, my emotional response might be anger.

Anger might occur with the picture cards hand vs. hand (12); or back stabbing (58).

The emotion of disgust: To the word cards ROT, FAIL, SELF-DEFEATING, SHAME, SLAVE, HATE, DISGRACE or GUILT, I might respond with disgust.

Disgust might occur with the picture cards man in corner (68); axe in hand (36); screamer (46); hand chopped off (47); twister (1); outcast (55); and spilled milk (4).

The emotion of pleasure: My emotional response to the word cards COMIC, FASCINATION, GAME, HOME, WONDERFUL, MOTHER, JOY or LAUGHTER might be pleasure.

Pleasure might be the emotion I experience with the picture cards couple on beach (43); tree (53); fireplace (76); dancers (67); food (74); monastery (30); study hall (66); rainbow (38); bird (29); Sun (39); seashore (34); forest (48); the hug (77); playground (45); clown (88); or nursing (25).

The emotion of fear: When I encounter such cards as INTIMIDATE,

BOSS, DANGER, CONFUSION, VICTIM, VIOLATE, PAIN or FEAR, my response might be fear.

Fear might also be my reaction to the picture cards of the cat in front of the cave (27); snake (51); masked person (16), skeleton (54); storm (87); whirlpool (14); pole/twisted (20); and patient (26).

The emotion of surprise: DREAM, LOVE, CHANGE, EROTIC, GO, LETTING GO, RETREAT or JOY are word cards that might engender my surprise.

Surprise might also be my reaction to the picture cards of the key in the door (22); cards (6); altar (42); underwater diver (71); dead end (40); stairway (18); slap on the face (31).

It is clear from practice with the OH Cards that any card can elicit any emotion. For instance, the picture of the naked male genitals (picture card 57) would cause loss of restraint in a person who lacks self-control; disgust in some cultural groups; fear in a woman who fantasizes about being raped; desire in one who delights in sex; or envy in one who is impotent.

What is essential to know about the cards which are drawn is that an emotional response is a wake-up call from the unconscious and is a matter for conscious consideration.

Following is a personal account of a woman who is a teacher. She is in a group which meets regularly and often uses the OH Cards. She called this experience with the OH Cards an "emotional roller coaster." Her comments are included with her permission as an illustration of the emotional impact OH Card usage may have.

Her description starts first with an encounter she had with a student she was trying to get through to in counseling. Her second encounter was with herself. She concluded with her overall observations.

An encounter with a student. *Since we know the OH Cards have always proved accurate for us, I'm trying to recall those incidents where the accuracy really took me aback. One such incident is of course when I was counseling a young man at a local high school. He had just returned from a two-day suspension for slugging out another kid in one of his classes, and for cursing at a cafeteria teacher. This was a very closed individual and I was attempting to get him in touch with his feelings.*

I kept referring to the fact that he had a lot of anger within him, which he kept denying. I asked him if he would be interested in laying out some OH Cards to which he agreed. I said, "Let's put a card down for the feeling inside – I keep calling those feelings anger, but that's unfair of me because you're telling me that you don't feel anger, so we'll just call this card your feelings."

Sure enough, when we turned that particular card over, the word was "anger." He still didn't understand this anger, but he no longer denied it.

An encounter with myself. *We also know that what is occurring on the inside will be symbolically represented in the outer. This is what happened to me after a group session. We each drew an OH card which represented ourselves, mine being the card of exclusion.* (picture card 55)

This upset me and began a whirlwind of psychic energy around me. When I returned home, I received upsetting news from school which made me feel excluded from the rest of the class. I attempted to go to the high school to finish up the testing I was doing on one of the students and arrived to find all the cars gone out of the parking lot. The school had suffered a power outage, and everyone was sent home. Again I felt an exclusion.

I decided to drive to the supermarket to get groceries since I now had free time I hadn't planned on. On the car radio, callers were talking about their lack of fulfillment in life with marriage, but most people are better off married, and for women it was mostly for financial reasons, not necessarily emotional fulfillment. This left me with another void in my feelings. After filling up my cart and now waiting in the checkout line, the clerk, whom I had noticed to be a middle-aged woman (because the thought had crossed my mind, "Oh, the middle-aged women work during the day, and the high school kids work in the evenings") finished the customer in front of me and, just before starting my items, burst into tears at the cash register and called for backup on the phone to the desk. Another female cashier came and whisked the tearful clerk away.

My feelings were being played out for me in front of my eyes – another middle-aged woman excluded from society, a throwaway population.

MY OBSERVATIONS ABOUT THESE EXPERIENCES. *One must be prepared for the feelings and events that the OH Cards may stir up. It you are really serious about using the OH Cards, be prepared for the torrent of feelings that can follow. These were stirring readings which I can recall vividly off the top of my head. Both of these illustrate how accurate and powerful the OH Cards can be. For those who are receptive to it, I plan on using OH Cards in my therapy work. And, of course, I'll continue to consult them for personal guidance.*

As illustrated above, the OH Cards can be used in the tradition of Carl G. Jung who proposed in his writings that existing symbols could be used instead of waiting for symbols to emerge from the unconscious through dreams. An advantage of using the OH Cards is that the images of the picture cards are universal and, along with the word cards, suggest different meanings at different times. This allows them to fit into the varying situations and experiences of the persons using them.

These experiences of the teacher illustrate that each category of a life experience is tempered by an emotion. The level of emotion, like a condiment added to food to give it flavor, ranges from bland to overpowering. In both readings above, the wake-up call was represented by one card. Anger (word card 91) had special impact in the situation with the student and for the group member it was picture card 55. In the first encounter, through the OH Cards, the young student has been able to acknowledge the anger within himself. In the second encounter the teacher has discovered her own personal inner angst.

The OH Cards have allowed self-realization both for the teacher and the student. They each have been shown a truth about an area of controversy within themselves. This will open up each of them to the possibility of understanding the factors contributing to their turmoil and the accommodations they may be able to make to deal with the disturbances in their lives.

Every OH consultation will contain some emotion, sometimes only slight and sometimes a mixture of several emotions. The same card does not produce the same emotion for everyone. What is felt is unique to the individual. There may be an immediate bodily reaction, perhaps an adrenalin rush, elation, or sadness.

These are the same kinds of emotional responses which arise from everyday happenings such as when the bank takes money from your account by mistake or your child is sent home from school for misbehaving. The deeper the encounter with the OH Cards, the more intensive will be the emotions and the greater will be the likelihood of dealing with important life decisions.

USING OH TO UNDERSTAND PERSONAL PSYCHOLOGY

During my childhood, I received the gift of a Ouija board. With a Ouija board it is plausible to think up an answer and will it to be spelled out. This is the performance of a conscious act. It will result in an answer from the conscious, not from the unconscious. If the planchette is deliberately maneuvered, again it is the conscious mind controlling the response.

On the other hand, thoughts, actions, and behavior do not influence the outcome of the cards drawn at random from the picture and word decks of the OH Cards because randomly selecting cards is not a mental process and does not involve logic.

I have traveled far beyond the germinal experience with the Ouija board and, in the years which have followed, I have been working to create a dialogue between the unconscious and the conscious using symbolic forms as the language. The examples of the teacher and her student in the earlier chapter illustrate the value of the pictures and words in bringing to the surface information from the psyche in the process of self-discovery and self-revelation.

It is important for persons to know themselves and their characteristics. It will also help them to accept their idiosyncracies and their peculiarities without shame or disgust. This is important for growth and balance.

Carl Jung said that psychotherapy is worthless for persons who do not have an understanding of their personal psychology. For example, during adolescence, I exhibited a great deal of cynicism. Thus it is fair to say that my psychology at the time was *based in cynicism.*

Since I was so cynical, I can tell you some things about the adolescent cynic. A cynic has difficulties with self-acceptance. For example, cynical adolescents reject such things as how they look even though they look fine. They also avoid competing with peers. They are critical of others and are always knocking them. To them everything is profane, especially if value is attached to an experience or an object. Their favorite pastime is destroying the peace wherever it is found. This they accomplish by giving everyone they meet advice on all subjects.

One whose psychology is based in cynicism is masking his sense of an inability to compete. Until I found out about my cynicism I could not drop this sense of an inability to compete. The reason I know this psychology so well is because I have lived the experience. A contrasting experience is that of a friend who is a mathematician; his psychology is *based in regimentation.* He is practical in every sense of the word. He does not allow for experimentation into his unconscious. If it is not something available to one of his five senses, he is not interested in it.

He and his wife are having marital problems. The beginning of the end came several years ago when they were vacationing. His wife wanted to sightsee and he wanted to sit at cafés and bars. He says that he realized then that they did not belong together.

Persons whose psychology is based in regimentation are masking the inability to be spontaneous. When he sought out a wife, he found a mate who was similarly regimented. His father had been very regimented also. When something comes up for the first time, such as a desire to sit around cafés in Paris and be spontaneous, it is preceded by infantile material which was forgotten long ago. Such persons were deprived of a childhood. Their aberrations may take them into adolescent behavioral patterns such as a predilection for an affair or a sudden urge just to bum around, simply engaging in what appears to be aimless activity. When the thought of being spontaneous came to him, his wife, being his mirror-image, rejected it. He is unaware of the fact that he is really seeking to balance his psychological state.

Regimentation-based psychology does not allow for play. Therefore when play occurs it must be done surreptitiously because the sense is that play is wrong. Until the person understands his individual psychology, it will not be possible to maintain a normal relationship with another. Being regimented 24 hours a day produces artificiality.

An acquaintance had her psychology *based in fear.* She could not view a scary movie nor could she enter a room with strangers without a sense of panic. Her favorite discussion subjects were the dark side and her shadow material.

She had been in psychotherapy for about two years when I knew her and, unfortunately, had not been able to grasp an understanding of where she was coming from. She knew about her fears and worked to get them into balance. Working to bring the pole of her fear into balance with the pole of courage is a good first step. The second step is in realizing that her psychology dominates and controls all aspects of her life just as regimentation does with the mathematician and as cynicism did with me.

Eventually, with her psychology based in fear, all her relationships crumble because the other person inevitably becomes the enemy, one who must be feared.

Regimentation excludes spontaneity. It masks the inability to let loose just as cynicism masks the inability to compete and just as fear masks the inability to enter into any relationship because eventually everyone becomes "the other," someone to be feared.

In like fashion, a psyche based in spontaneity, in courage, or in altruism, the opposites of fear and cynicism, would encounter similar obstacles to balance.

Neither extreme is good or bad. The goal is in bringing extremes into balance, at the same maintaining their unique distinctions so that neither extreme dominates.

Finding the dominant base is step one. Realizing its dominance is step two.

In order to deepen understanding of my own personal psychology, I drew three sets of OH Cards. SHAME (156), UGLY (167), and BOSS (100) were the word cards. The three picture cards were 65, the writing hand; 45, the playground; and 71, the snorkeler.

Shame describes the feeling a person has regarding any peculiarity he has. Cynicism is worn like a uniform. A cynic is easily spotted. As a teenager I had a job in a grocery store. One day the manager took me aside and handed me a piece of paper. On it were written the letters "c y n i c." I asked him what it meant. He told me to look it up in the dictionary. That evening, after I read the definition I saw that it was a perfect description of my attitude.

The next day I asked him why he had told me to look up the word. He replied, "Because you are a cynic." Fortunately I did not reject the suggestion. Rather I began a more thorough self-examination than I did for my weekly confession. The confessional was where I dealt with my venial and mortal sins, such as missing Mass on Sunday, or eating meat on Friday, or disobeying a parent. Looking at myself as a cynic opened me to a realization of who and what I was.

The picture card of the hand writing brings to mind the piece of paper with the letters "c y n i c."

The second word card, ugly, describes the pervasive nature of cynicism in my early life. It is as if I were breathing it in and breathing it out and taking it with me to work and school, or even to play, as the picture card shows.

The third word card, boss, describes my aspirations concerning my life. I want to know it and, to the extent possible, control it. I am swimming in the depths of my unconscious looking to discover aspects and energies of myself which direct and dominate me. These are the forces which propel me into certain behavioral patterns and attitudes.

As I have progressed in life in self-understanding, the rewards have grown. I have come to know about my deeper self.

If I approach life as a cynic I will not experience life in full measure. If my psychology is based in regimentation, I am living a half-life. If it is based in fear, it is less than that. My job is to educate myself about me. Using the OH Cards for self-examination and self-evaluation will guide me in choices and actions which are consistent with my personal path and the imprint upon life I aspire to make.

For the reader who does not have a grasp of his or her personal psychology, I have developed a simple exercise using the OH Cards. Think of the incident or ongoing experience which has caused you the greatest emotional turmoil. Whatever it may be – a relationship, an illness, a betrayal, the absence of another, a void – let the thought of it churn your being. Bring it to the fore. Hold on to the emotion. While you are in this state, take out the word cards from your OH Card decks and consciously select those which describe your experience and your feeling regarding the matter.

Try to do this when you are alone and not likely to be disturbed. Keep these cards separate and think about them for a few days. Take them into meditation. If another person is involved, sit in a chair across from an empty chair and image the other person sitting there. Show him or her the word cards you have selected. Tell the person how you feel.

Later that evening or the next day, pull out at random a corresponding number of picture cards and place them face down on the word cards. Turn them over one at a time. Open yourself to the teaching. This exercise should bring you to an understanding and a grasp of your own psychology.

The impact of the OH Cards is in how they work in tandem to generate the awakening of stored memories and a simultaneous emotional or physical reaction. At the same time they deal in the realm of innermost values and desires. OH brings attention to personal concerns and interests and reveals the meanings behind the true emotions.

Consulting the OH Cards is not a conscious process of applying logic and rationality. This would present a very biased picture influenced by personal filters. In everyday life, plans are developed and systematically executed. If life always went as planned, there would never be a need to turn within or pray to a God. It is not possible to mine the rich resources of the unconscious by applying conscious thought.

The application of OH is an unconscious process in which thinking has no bearing and rationalization is not a factor. Paths will open to the unconscious for symbolic revelation because drawing the OH Cards equates to the dream state.

The sleep state has nothing to do with the conscious functions of rationality and sophisticated mental functions such as planning or abstract thought. Logic and contextual memory are not the stuff of dreams. These originate in parts of the brain which are not active during sleep.

This explains why dreams have no coherence. Dreams play out in ornate scenarios filled with emotions and surprising images coupled with recent and long ago memories. They originate in the areas of the brain which are highly active in sleep; it is here that emotion, memory formation, motivation and auditory and visual data make their homes.

There is no order in the sequence of images within the dream and time does not exist in the dream. Nor is there self-awareness. Such a state is opposite to the world of consciousness in which events appear to come into existence prompted by predecessor happenings. In the world of the unconscious there is no cause and effect and there are no successor events. Free will which appears to exist in the conscious realm is absent here. Use of the OH Cards does not involve a rational process because cards are drawn at random, an unconscious act.

The inner self is ordinarily so distant and so complex that it is beyond the reach of the conscious mind except as it is revealed in dreams. OH Cards are an especially effective means because it is the very same area of the brain where dreams occur which is engaged in usage of the OH Cards.

OH BIRTHDAY CARDS

Birthdays have always been a special day for me to reflect upon my life. The anniversary of the date of my birth serves as a moment in time each year for me to revisit myself. It is an opportunity to commune with myself and to do inventory, exploration, and renewal. From the time of my discovery of OH several years ago and on each birthday since, I celebrate – and give myself some OH Birthday Cards.

The conscious and the unconscious cohabit in the psyche but each exists in a separate world with a separate language – images for the unconscious and words for the conscious. Before OH, my look at myself and into these realms was as if through a glass darkly, as St. Paul said.

OH is a tool that communicates with both realms simultaneously and brings them to my awareness because it encompasses both pictures and words. OH Cards operate in the psyche like an airbag in an automobile which balloons into action whenever the car has a sudden impact. In somewhat the same manner, OH Cards impact upon the person who uses them, activating innate energies which express as emotions, intuitions, feelings, fantasy images, ideas, and motifs and bringing them to the surface of awareness.

A reading I performed upon myself on a recent birthday illustrates how the use of OH can be helpful in self-examination. The six cards – three word cards and three picture cards – which I drew at random were apropos to my purpose.

I began my reading by shuffling each deck of the OH Cards. Then, I drew three word cards at random. I turned them over in this order – FATHER (120); CYCLE (107); HOPE (135).

Then I drew three picture cards and, in order, they were number 56 (a *doctor*); number 72 (a *nurse*); and number 19 (a *bedroom*)

Following the same order in which I originally drew them, I placed the picture cards on the word cards – doctor (56) on father; nurse (72) on cycle; bedroom (19) on hope.

The doctor in picture card 56 is performing my annual physical. It equates to the present action in which I am involved as I consult OH for my annual self-examination.

The Word Card FATHER *and* Picture Card 56

The doctor is performing his examination using medical diagnostic tools just as I am using OH as an examination tool for my reading. On his head the doctor wears a mirror-like disk which reflects and also focuses light through a hole in the center. This represents a principle in optics known as the pinhole effect because the light passes through the hole in a straight line. Diffuse light can obscure the view and too much light can blind the observer. However, the light through the pinhole provides acuity of vision, 20/20. The learning here is to stay narrowly focused in order to see the details keenly and acutely.

The disk on the doctor's head looks like a third eye, symbolizing the eye of spiritual perception and which is sometimes called the eye of the heart. The doctor uses the stethoscope to listen to the rhythm of my heart beating and to hear the passage of air in and out of my lungs. The symbolism of this tool points to utilizing my ability to comprehend and understand the rhythms of life. My attention is also drawn to an observation of Tom Chetwynd in *Dictionary of Symbols* in his discussion of animus as a masculine figure in the woman's psyche. He observed that the animus is also associated with problems with breathing such as asthma, which I developed in my adulthood. Perhaps this suggests a need for me to attend to matters of the anima.

A third tool is in the doctor's hand. It is a hammer which is used to test reflexes and to see that they are equal in intensity. The symbolism of this tool is that I am given the ability to discern the signatures of events which I observe or in which I participate.

The anticipated knee jerking from the tap of the doctor's hammer is the emotion I feel when an energy of my unconscious is excited and the hidden aspect concerning an event is being revealed. I note that the patient in the drawing is represented by two legs. This is very significant to me since during a three-year period in my childhood I could not use my left leg and my normal childhood activity was severely curtailed. Events come about in a manner designed to bring about a patterned outcome. Everything that happened to me – my premature birth, the paralysis of my leg, the gift of a Ouija board – conspired to bring me to where I am.

A doctor, when seen as one who has life in his hands, is a divine figure and I submit to his ministrations. A doctor's examination encompasses the entire body which is autonomous and which functions unconsciously. The doctor is imbued in science and is trained in a left-brained manner. Yet, the actual practice of medicine – a healing art – is very right-brained: It is intuitive, tactile, and visual-spatial. It is a symbol closely connected with the unconscious mind.

The companion word card is father. Father is masculine – the patriarch, the upholder of law and order, the voice of collective authority and, as lord over the material and temporal worlds, rules consciousness. In dreams, the father figure is the source of decisive convictions, prohibitions, and wise counsel. Father represents my consciousness, a statement of my expected orientation. The notion of "father" is contrary to instinctive impulse, spontaneous enthusiasm, and the unconscious.

I have a female side and a male side. My anima is my feminine side and my animus is my masculine side. The doctor/father combination forms my animus, the personification of my masculine thinking and of my masculine side in general. At the same time, it reflects my search for what is hidden and unknown through dreams and by instrumental means such as OH. The appearance of the doctor, who looms large as a godlike figure, is like a breath of the numen, a message from the Deity which resides within me. My animus identifies itself with God.

The Word Card CYCLE *and* Picture Card 72

The nurse (picture card 72) complements the doctor card. The nurse is garbed in the traditional uniform of nurses I recall from my childhood. She wears a stiffly starched white cap, white uniform, and a nursing school pin. The helpmate of the doctor, the nurse suggests attendance and service.

The nurse is a significant symbol to me and transports me to the time of my infancy. Mine was not a full term birth and as a result I spent the first weeks of my life in the hospital. Because I was born two months prematurely, my mother's visits to me were limited. The source of much of the care, nurturing, and love I received during the first few weeks of my life was from a nurse.

My mother had intended naming me Ronald. She liked the actor Ronald Colman and decided that if I were a male I would be Ronald. Before she could bestow his name upon me, a woman in the next bed chose Ronald to name her baby. My mother, not wanting to be thought of as a copycat named me Donald instead. This did not change my mother's unconscious wish that she wanted her son to be like the actor, who was successful, suave, handsome, articulate, and romantic and played roles of characters who were wholesome and forthright.

My mother's milk was brought to the hospital on a daily basis by my grandfather, Ben, and was fed to me by the nurse. Even as a duck hatched from an egg by a chicken will adopt the hen as its mother and will behave in all respects like the baby chicks, my archetypal mother figure was a white nurse even though my birth mother was an African-American woman.

The naming process is a fixing, a creation, and is more than giving a person or an event a name. The name is the archetypal identification and does not necessarily include the actual giving of a name. For example, the first occurrence of something or an event can become the model for all succeeding such events which have the same ingredients, much as the first cake made in a certain way will fix the taste of all cakes similarly made thereafter.

My true "naming" process took place not when my mother moved from

Ronald to Donald. My identification – my naming - was with this starched white figure who fed me my mother's milk. My mother and the nurse, a mother-figure, symbolize the idea of the Dual Mother – in this case my early formation was of the worlds of different races. This early experience was to impact upon me later.

My personal introduction to race consciousness happened while I was studying for the priesthood in Bay St. Louis, Mississippi at the seminary of the Society of the Divine Word, the German Order which ran the school. An attack of acute appendicitis while I was at the seminary during my teen years jolted me from my fantasy. Thanks to a dose of Milk of Magnesia® administered by the Prefect, my appendix ruptured and I was in a life-threatening predicament. The nearest hospital was in Biloxi but it was for white people only; I had to travel 90 miles to New Orleans, to find a hospital which would admit me. The priest who accompanied me on the train could not sit with me on the trip. I was in the colored section and then after that I sat in the back of the city streetcar on the final leg of my trip to the hospital.

The experience struck me like a thunderbolt. I learned that I was not a sick boy. I was a sick boy of a different race and this fact had life and death significance. The CYCLE word card awakens a primal energy; the reenactment of creation over and over is a source of strength. The power is in the cycling process. The naming is the creation, the triggering, the bringing into existence.

The Rabbis teach that the Sabbath exists before creation, that cycle precedes matter. The cycle of creation is itself an indefinable process, one that does not partake of the physical universe whereas everything in the physical universe does partake of the process. Everything in the cosmos is of the Creation.

The nurse as pictured is a no-nonsense character, one who enforces the rules without the influence of emotionality. In other words the cycle will not be altered. There will be no changes within the cycle's formula. Yet over her heart chakra there is a red medal, symbolizing universal love, the love without condition. I recall my childhood devotion to the Sacred Heart of Mary, coincidentally my mother's name. My mother was devout and regularly prayed novenas to Our Lady of Sorrows.

The doctor symbolizes the male energy, the nurse the female energy, indicating the wholeness of my existence. Like the doctor/father, the combination nurse/cycle is a numen, a message from the Goddess within me. This message is wisdom, the *Sapientia* of the Goddess. Now the Deity is no longer split or separated. My anima identifies itself with the Goddess and I am now balanced.

The process of moving from a beginning to an end is a cycle – a circle with action and inaction moving through time. By comparing cycles, I evaluate life with the aim of creating one contiguous whole. In the modern world, most basic survival instincts have been suppressed and some have been annihilated. The need to identify with the processes of life is glaring. The nurse and cycle remind me of the aspects which affect my life. It is through this knowledge that I will have liberation.

The Word Card HOPE *and* Picture Card 19

The final word card is HOPE. The picture card (19) is of a bedroom. The bed is covered with a green spread and the sheet and bedspread are folded back in readiness for me to lie down. There are a pair of green-covered pillows, a green throw rug and green drapes. The floor is neat, as if just sanded. There is a green plant on the windowsill. Under the bed are two pairs of shoes.

The bed is like a launching pad into the world of dreams, into another dimension. Once I go to sleep the unconscious takes over and begins its nightly transmissions of information from the unconscious to the conscious. This is a necessary function for life. The conscious me needs the unconscious me in order to function and survive even as my left brain and my right brain, which are physical manifestations of the conscious and the unconscious, need each other in order for the brain to function fully.

The two pairs of shoes under the bed continue the representation of male and female energies. Shoes are worn on the feet, which are the lowest part of the physical body. The feet represent the lower human aspects such as physical and emotional pleasures. Since they clothe the feet, shoes symbolize lower desires and bodily passions. Thus, when Moses is standing at the burning bush he is told to take off his shoes because the place where he is standing is holy ground. (*Exodus* 3:2-5) The significance of this is that before he can move into a state where he can communicate with his inner being, his unconscious, Moses must divest himself of physical desires and passions – drop his earthbound conscious self which is governed by the left brain and move wholly into his right brain, the world of dreams and imagery. He is being called upon to bring balance to his outlook.

The bed also signifies the alpha and omega of life itself, birth and death, the place of coming and going. As the place of the ritual of sex, the bed is also the altar of creativity.

All of us perform rituals in work, play, and prayer. The ritual in turn triggers the unconscious. An example: A professional basketball player shooting a free throw performs a ritual. He always does it in exactly the same way. Some players, like Charles Barkley, will caress the ball lovingly. John Starks will stare into space before putting the basket in focus. There are players who will bounce the ball a specific number of times or others who will contort their faces in the same way each time. All of these shooting rituals numb the conscious mind much as does a mantra for one who would go into the meditative state. As easy as it seems, shooting a free throw should be as simple as dribbling for a player. Yet the percentages for making free throws vary significantly. The players with the consistent ritual shoot better free throws than those who do not have such a ritual.

When the unconscious is synchronous with the conscious, when the right brain is in harmony with the left brain, the effects are immediately noticeable. The importance of the ritual is the increased activity and practical use of the unconscious. It is one of the most successful methods of keeping the unconscious and conscious united and working together.

The color green is significant here for its symbolism. Green is a comforting color. After the isolation and desolation of winter, the arrival of spring clothes the earth in green, bringing HOPE – which is the word card – and making it again the nurse of the human race. Just as plant life draws its energy from the Sun in the process of photosynthesis so, too, does the conscious self draw its energy from the activities of the unconscious. Energy promotes growth, healing, renewal, and regeneration.

The bed has a special significance for me. It was when I was beridden and crippled that I received the gift of a Ouija board. Ouija became, just as OH, the vehicle which formed a bridge between conscious Adam and unconscious Adam. When later I was once again able to walk, my parents, the priest, and nuns, all called it a miracle. When a person with Savant Syndrome plays classical music or does complicated math, no one calls it a miracle. My healing and that music both sprang from within, from the unconscious, a universal source of power and knowledge.

Overview of My OH Birthday Cards

Consideration of the cards begins with the associations which first come to mind. Perhaps there is some relationship to a recent event or a current situation. Perhaps the connection is to some early experience that has an impact in the present. If the cards involve the use of several pairs of word and picture cards, many different associations will spring to mind as occurred with the cards which I drew on my birthday.

Answers and memories are triggered by associations and reminiscences and within them I look for similarities and matches. The common aspects will jump to the surface. Apart from the ordinary meanings of the words and the images, the cards and the extra meanings drawn from them will express my characteristics as they did in my discussion of what the OH Cards reflected back to me and the perspective they helped me to formulate.

The OH Cards which affect my emotions are the ones to which I pay particular attention – like that jolt of awareness I had when I was at the seminary. The quickening of the pulse, or the fast breathing, or the rapid heartbeat, or even perspiration are typical signals which pinpoint matters of importance. Sometimes emotions are especially troubling. I can learn to handle the emotion in an OH reading or any encounter if I remember that the cause of the disturbance is not in the outer event or in the person who might appear to be the cause. The disturbance which I experience relates to my inner life.

What I have written about my "birthday cards" is what I call a reading. It does not mean that my interpretation of the cards relates in any way to another person who happens to draw the same cards. Human beings share a collective unconscious. However, each of us has an individual unconscious which is unique; mine gives the cards my meanings.

Thus, on my birthday I have taken a measure of my life. I have been presented with a look at the influence of my experiences upon my life on this date. I am a person who seeks a deeper analysis of everything I encounter including myself. I walk at ease in all ethnic, racial, and religious worlds. I make no identification of myself because of an exterior feature. Ritual is critical for me. I engage in a studied ritual designed by me which engages my creative talents. Understanding rhythms and cycles is very important to me. I want to know where I fit and live according to that model.

I cannot define myself until and unless I have fully explored my unconscious, its expressions, its urges, and its patterning and can express these in conscious symbols. The phenomenon which can accomplish such a task is to engage the unconscious as I did with the OH Cards on my birthday. The images which Ely Raman painted bear his imprint. Nevertheless, I find meanings in them which relate to me. The analysis which I can make of an artist's material is exactly comparable to the method I apply to consideration of the OH Cards. This reading I performed on myself with the OH Cards on my birthday is a benchmark in the unfolding of my life.

REACHING THE DEPTHS WITH OH

When I began work with the OH Cards, I tried at first to establish a singleness of meaning for each of the picture and word cards. This I soon found out misses the essential point. The one sure thing about the picture cards is that they trigger manifold meanings, depending on the individual response.

The OH picture cards and word cards exemplify the symbolic process of the unconscious at work They present an experience in images reflecting the very basic notion that fixed deep in the human psyche is a milieu of primary figures, pictures, and schemata. We recognize this in other species. Simple examples are the inborn response of a kitten to pursue a mouse at first sight; the instinctive fear a pigeon has upon sight of a paper silhouette of an owl; the instinct of both human and animal to flee from the danger of fire.

The particular significance of the OH word cards is their ability to excite and to stir the conscious mind. Words, both written and spoken, are the progeny of the onset and development of humans as conscious beings. Some of the OH word cards are descriptive, deceptively so, since at first impression they seem to express only one surface meaning. Deeper probing will always reveal alternatives. Other words are action oriented. Yet even these have multiple meanings as words adopt hybrid definitions and alternate usages. As parts of speech, nouns become verbs, verbs become nouns, and both become adjectives.

The mythological story in *Genesis* (Chapter 11) of a single language among all people has seemed improbable to most people. Recent studies suggest that the Biblical version may be a possibility after all. The unifying feature of a tribe, a nation, or a colony of ants is its uniform method of communication.

The unconscious has always had a universal tongue. The collective ideas which are shared by all humankind and the primordial images which they express are part and parcel of life itself. Like all languages, these collective ideas have expanded and formed over the centuries. They condition us; they govern our thought processes; they tell us about the world we live in. Whenever I attempt to solve a problem, they influence the outcome. Attitudes are shaped by these collective ideas. They influence our conceptions of God, life and death, parents and siblings.

In a creation myth of the Vedas, an androgynous primal man separated and became a man and a woman and from the man and woman came the world and with it dualism was created. Another well-known creation myth tells of the separation of the cosmic egg into a male sky and a female earth. Eve owes her existence to Adam. Duality expresses throughout all of nature in a recurrent theme, a rhythm of life/death, here/hereafter, good/evil, mind/matter, sacred/profane, negative/positive, dark/light, happy/sad, saint/sinner, stop/go, order/chaos, with masculine/feminine being the most elemental and fundamental.

The picture cards and the word cards in combination give expression to the dualism of the conscious and the unconscious. The result is that lines between the conscious and the unconscious open up in much the same way as in a dream. There is no right or wrong, only meaning which is flowing from the unconscious and is the expression of this particular moment.

Using the OH Cards is a discussion with the unconscious. When I am not using them, the discussion continues. Once activated by using the word and picture cards, the flow continues unabated without use of the cards. Once I have begun the process with the OH Cards, sudden insights will have more meaning.

For instance, while I am speaking, the unconscious is preparing my next sentence. When the unconscious is not functioning or cooperating, I pause midpoint to await what comes next. If a person whose name I should know walks up to me at a party, my unconscious supplies the person's name. My conscious mind does not store data. The unconscious collaborates with the conscious and gives me what I need – I say "It's on the tip of my tongue" or I thought of it "right off the top of my head."

Getting at the information stored in memory is an ancient problem of humankind. In Paleolithic times, early humans kept records in the form of notches in bone, horn, and stone, burn marks on skin and hide, and knots on string. Memory aides in use today range from notes on paper napkins to electronic storage devices.

Thomas Bayes, an eighteenth-century mathematician, devised an algebraic formula. It is called the Bayes' theorem of subjective probability and what it does is to quantify the value of a hunch – to factor in the knowledge which is beyond the conscious mind and which is in the unconscious.

Bayes' theorem was successfully applied by a team of mathematicians in 1966 to recover an H-bomb lost in a mid-air collision between a B-52 bomber and a refueling tanker. The bomb was found in a ravine 2,550 feet below the surface of the Mediterranean, a location which went against all conscious logic because it was far from where most of the plane's debris had hit the water and far from where three other bombs had been found.

When an irrational process produces a right answer, a rational person asks how this could be possible. When a rational person gets a rational answer from an irrational process it is disturbing. The temptation is to repeat the question to see if it works a second time. A rational person who does this has become irrational and the irrational approach produces more irrationality.

That a response which makes sense would come out of what appears to be an unconnected act of pulling cards from two decks is a phenomenon. It works over and over because you have entered the *invisible* side of yourself. There is no need to dissect the process. If you think of the *visible* in mathematical terms as a plus (+) and the invisible world as a minus (-), it is easy to see how the plus and the minus harmonize without either losing its identity. Symbols serve as the mediator between the visible and the invisible.

Jung wrote that the unconscious thinks and lives in terms of millennia and when we think we have a new discovery, "it is generally a very old story indeed." Solomon, the reputed author of *Ecclesiastes* wrote: "History merely repeats itself. Nothing is truly new; it has all been done or said before. What can you point to that is new? How do you know it didn't exist long ages ago? We don't remember what happened in those former times, and in the future generations no one will remember what we have done back here." (*Ecclesiastes* 1:8)

Because "we don't remember," we ponder the wonders from antiquity such as the Great Pyramid of Giza and question how this masterpiece of technical skill and engineering ability could have been built without modern technology. Its sides rise at an angle of 51° 52' and the pyramid is accurately oriented to the four cardinal points of the compass. There have been numerous theories about how it was done, including the strongly held belief that Earth was visited by beings from other solar systems who supervised its construction.

The tendency of persons is to look outside of themselves or to fantasize a visit from an extraterrestrial to explain what they cannot fathom with their conscious understanding. The unconscious holds solutions to the needs of an individual or a group, whether a tribe or a nation, even for a species of ants. The genius and know-how which are being sought exist within the psyche in the storehouse of the unconscious – the realm of all wisdom and knowledge. It is here that universal and transcendent forms or archetypes reside which exist across time, space, and species. The archetypes of the unconscious preexist us and are an inexhaustible wellspring embedded within the human psyche like diamonds deep in kimberlite pipes, waiting to be mined.

There is saying among the Rabbis that asks, "Have you ever seen a beast or a fowl that had a workshop?" The concept is one also expressed by Jesus. The teachings of Jesus in the Sermon on the Mount advising his followers to place trust in the providence of God with issues of life could very well be a discussion about the unconscious.

Jesus was preaching symbolically. (*Matthew* 6:25-33) His teachings were plain and about the familiar and referred to birds and to the lilies growing wild in the fields. Jesus' message was that every creature and all of creation are in their existence what God, (substitute the unconscious) has made it possible for them to be. This expresses the meaning of the unconscious as the source of every single thing human beings may ever need to achieve perfection. Similarly in *Psalms 23*: "The Lord (substitute the unconscious) is my shepherd, I shall not want."

In the ancient language of India known as *Sanskrit,* the word for the verb "to be" shares the same root form with the verb "to grow." Growth is a necessary component of existence. This is the dynamic of the unconscious as an endless resource to support survival from one generation to the next.

The unconscious has access to data which is closed to the conscious. Physical facts and events are mere shadows of the reality of these facts and events. A coin flipped into the air or a box of matches thrown on the floor have features I cannot detect with my conscious mind. The coin will have an angle, a trajectory, a side preference, a smoothness, or a flaw, and these aspects plus a hundred others will affect the coin's landing.

A person who is mentally disabled and exhibits Savant Syndrome can look at the matches on the floor and tell you how many there are. He does not count them consciously. His unconscious does it and passes along the answer. In other such individuals, islands of genius may be the ability to perform map memorizing, or in others the ability for perfect appreciation of time passing without knowledge of a clock face. Musical ability is the most common exceptional talent among those with Savant Syndrome. Whatever the special skills, they are always linked with phenomenal memory, deep and narrow, which relies upon more primitive circuitry. Obviously they arise from the unconscious realm.

I once met a five-year-old boy who could spell any word and he could also do complicated math problems. Mozart at age three could play chords on the harpsichord and short pieces by the time he was four years old. By the age of five, he was composing concertos. Whether it is an Einstein or a Picasso or an Edison – or a child prodigy – it is the unconscious which is the source of genius, inventions, and innovations and of the feats of such precocious children.

When I consult the OH Cards, it is the unconscious which directs the draw of the cards. How does the unconscious see through the backs of cards? The answer is that neither sight nor any of the other senses exists in the unconscious; they are not needed. Different forms of sight, touch, smell, hearing, and tasting exist in the unconscious.

Eventually I come to understand that the things I do are in most respects based on a preformed system of instincts: Thought forms, reflexes, attitudes, images, and gestures are the same the world over. Everyone starts life with the same Original Myth, which is possessed by all people who have ever lived and who have used it to make sense of their world and their place in it.

Every function I perform, such as Mother, Father, or Child, and every behavioral pattern I exhibit, such as Worker, Soldier, or Nurse, has a history. All began with an event, something which originally was done or accomplished eons ago, well beyond human history. These first events and patterns of behavior are our archetypes. These first time accomplishments became the molds by which all subsequent behavior came to be fashioned.

Within the collective unconscious are sets of blueprints detailing precisely how every role in life is to be played out and how every action is to be performed. These universal primordial images are inborn in the psyche of every human being, meaning that all of this data comes with the territory, so to speak, and is a given. At conception, I know all there is to know about the roles expressed by these archetypes.

While the number of different roles and actions which are our archetypes cannot be calculated, remarkably there are only six basic categories of archetypes. These six divide into three male or active archetypes and three female or passive archetypes. The three female archetypes are corollaries of the three male archetypes.

The male archetypes are the Survival archetype, the Territorial archetype, and the Power archetype. The female archetypes are the Relationship archetype, the Service archetype, and the Dependence archetype. They are as their names indicate and they pair up as Power/Relationship; Territorial/Service; and Survival/Dependence.

Violence is native to the three male archetypes. No matter what excuse or label is attached to the violence, the actor's ultimate cause derives from the need to survive, a quest for more territory, or a desire for more power. Guile is native to the female archetypes, again without regard to the reason assigned by the actor.

The six archetypes are activated in all beings at conception. The sex of the actors does not matter: Both the masculine and the feminine of all species are created with a full complement of all six archetypes. Leafcutter ants provide an example to illustrate this: While most of the ants are female, nonetheless in various stages all six of the archetypes manifest in all the ants.

Although the female archetypes operate through guile and the male archetypes through violence, this does not mean that female archetypes do not arise in masculine beings and that the male archetypes do not arise in the feminine beings. All archetypes arise in all beings: All males of all species have all six archetypes as do all females of all species.

The sexual act provides an illustration. The female of the human species craves foreplay and intimacy. The male is centered on intercourse. Thus the male will engage in foreplay and intimacy to the extent necessary in order to get the female to surrender. For the male, the act of intercourse is an exercise of the Power archetype. For the female, getting the male to become intimate fulfills the Relationship archetype. Thus she uses guile in order to draw the male into something more permanent than the base act of sexual intercourse could ever produce.

The male is driven to exercise his Power archetype and if his female counterpart will not allow him to do so, he will overcome her will, either with gifts or by force. Thus there have occurred the concepts of rape and prostitution.

The three male archetypes are also exercised by females, usually in a different style. The female Dependence archetype is exercised by her in order to achieve the Survival archetype. The Survival archetype equates with want, desire, aggression, and determination whereas a feminine archetype such as Relationship corresponds to achievement by persuasion through temptation, even with guile.

Dividing the archetypes into masculine and feminine distinguishes the active (masculine) resolve or *agens*. Alchemically it would be regarded as the *upwelling*. The feminine archetype is the *patiens*, the receptive, the aspect of whatever eventually manifests, that which is still to be formed.

Like the six quarks which are the basic foundation of matter the six archetypes are a unity. The quarks and the archetypes act as a whole and my entire psyche and my conscious system move instantaneously and simultaneously together with a single purpose.

At some point in my years of self-examination and scrutiny I have asked myself, "Why?" Would it not be simpler just to live out my life like others around me, satisfied with whatever temporal pleasures are at hand? Instead, something within drove me, more or less on my own, to a place of knowledge of self and how I tick. Armed with this knowledge, I arrived at an understanding of what I call *Patterning*. This understanding has enriched me as no earthly treasure ever could.

Patterning is a powerful force. It points the individual onto a path; it points the tribe or racial group into a recognizable culture; it points the nation into a role; and finally it points the world itself on to certain goals or destinies. The human nature I share is because of a single gene pool and because of the collective unconscious which I have in common with the generation in which I live and with the generations before me and which will follow after me.

The unconscious is an obscure realm and is cloaked in mystery. Access to its information involves a process of demystification – realizing that I can come to know my patterning through symbols, images, and by analogy. Understanding the process lies in awareness that at one point in the cycle of human existence, words and images clashed and words won. A defining moment of the battle is illustrated at Sinai when Moses came down from the top of the mountain after forty days only to find that the Hebrew people had collected the golden jewelry in the camp, melted it down, and sculpted themselves a golden calf to worship. Moses was bringing words; the people were engaging images. Perhaps the people missed participating in rituals in the land they had left behind. Ritual and image work a magic which words alone cannot do.

Moses was carrying two very large tablets upon which God had written his commandments, the parameters by which the people were going to live their new lives. What a shock it must have been for him! He had been in a transcendent state for the previous forty days communing with the God who had protected these people and here they were violating the first two of God's commandments: The bans on other gods and on graven images.

For me, such a struggle epitomizes the underlying push and pull between the conscious and the unconscious. The spoken and written words of the conscious unwittingly were thrown into a conflict with the pictures and images of the unconscious.

When they are in conflict, both the conscious and the unconscious are distorted. Alone, the conscious produces endless wars and emphasis on one side or the other of the extremes. Alone, the unconscious moves into its extremes of superstition and sexual excess and abuse.

When they are in balance, one to the other, the conscious and the unconscious are harmonized. There is always a third solution in addition to merely living or dying. In order to find that way, I engage both aspects of my being. Eventually I come to understand that world peace begins with me. I am of the cosmos and my every thought and my every action affect the cosmos and therefore are of consequence.

In keeping with this cosmic sense of duality, I have two different images of my self. The question which concerns me is whether or not the split between my consciousness and the unconscious lies as this cause of this duality. The answer is that my sense of duality was present at my conception. I always was the way that I am.

It is in understanding this truth that I begin the process of balancing the light of my consciousness with the darkness of my unconscious. For, according to St. Augustine, every spiritual truth turns into something material.

The OH Cards are a tool to assist me in working towards a balance between these dual worlds of being, between masculine words and feminine images. The goal is to engage both aspects of my being, my conscious and my unconscious. Both realms are legitimate and necessary for the full experience of life and all of the antecedents present at birth.

When I use the OH Cards, I am opening the door to the unconscious and bringing myself to the full presence of my psyche. The messages which come forth are in the form of symbols. It is these symbols which are representative of the archetypes. A cow in a dream, for instance, could represent the Mother archetype; a jeep could represent the Father archetype; a toy scooter could represent the Child Archetype. The symbols in the OH Cards are as powerful as those in my dreams.

Interpreting most readings of the OH Cards requires no particular or special talent. No unusual study or knowledge is required. There are no tricks or artifices involved. It is common sense. I approach the deck as if I were sitting down for a meal to receive nourishment for a part of my being which ordinarily is shut out in my visible world. Dreams nourish me during my sleep. Try as they might, most people are not able to draw the meaning and message of the dream.

I have within myself certain characteristics which I keep hidden from others. Whenever they are brought to my consciousness they shock even me. The cards bring these things to the fore and compel me to look at those elements or forces which drive and define me.

In selecting cards I could have drawn any of several which could have spoken of these hidden individual qualities. Yet I have drawn the one which in this particular moment has a significance for me. It is *co-incident*, two events occurring at the same time, one in each realm.

There are times in interpreting the cards that it is as if I am speaking from within the cards. I put an "*I*" before the word card and read it as if I am the speaker. At other times, especially when it is a relationship question, it is as if the other person in the relationship is speaking. Sometimes I do not realize that I feel a certain way towards a person or a situation and the answer may surprise me. A lot depends on how I present the question. In any event, if I approach the process with a commitment to accept and abide by the answer and if I avoid frivolous and immature questions, I am much more likely to use the OH Cards successfully.

My experience with the OH Cards is that, rather than a static and repetitive result, there will be something new to be learned with every draw of the cards. A result is that *good advice* often comes out of the reading. Most times there are suggestions made which are rational and make sense.

Occasionally I do an inquiry on myself as I have previously demonstrated in this book. I examine my hidden, private aspects and through the OH Cards I am brought to the point where I am able to perceive and perform an *acknowledgment of my faults.*

Sometimes, when an opportunity arises for a new learning, perhaps to engage in a new program or occupation, what I derive from use of the OH Cards is the push or *the impetus* needed to get me started.

The child motif is prominent in many readings. When I understand that my feelings emerge from long past memories and do not relate to today's experiences, I can *divorce myself from the child motif.*

Difficulties arise. The OH Cards assist me in *surviving trauma.* Similarly, when either *adapting to good fortune* or *adapting to my losses*, the OH Cards can assist me.

With the word and picture cards I am inclined to *examine my belief system.*

Finally, OH Cards are a useful tool to guide me in *forming a philosophy of life.*

I commit myself to participate fully in a significant process of inquiry and to reap the rewards that come with understanding. I resist the temptation to keep things as they are and open myself to the possibility of bringing my unconscious into a harmonious communication with my conscious. I recall the teachings of the Sermon on the Mount and its allusions and apply the lessons of these symbols to my own life.

Working with the OH Cards is a path to growth, insight, and appreciation of self and others. For me, this is the value, worth, and reward of OH.

PART II

Picture Card 1

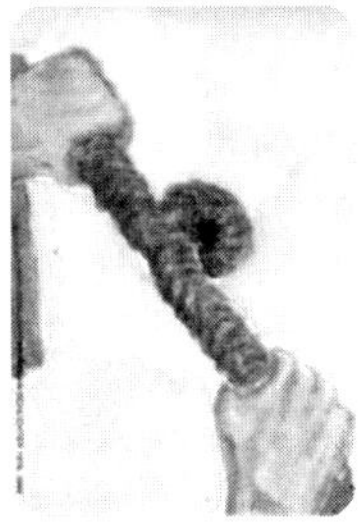

To twist something is to distort it. If it is straight, twisting bends and misshapes it. If it is curved, twisting warps it. Hands express the attitude of the person. Held upward they denote surrender. One hand held upward means peace. A fist in the air expresses belligerence. Hands represent action. Here they are the means of applying the force. How I describe this image is a factor of my emotions. Anger? Frustration? Anxiety?

My intuitive skills guide me in interpreting this card. This card is an expression of great tension. Is this an image of tension which needs to be held in balance? The tension in wringing is so intense that the coil, which represents the central nervous system or the spine, has begun to twist. When I see the knot as being formed, it means enslavement, insult, or humiliating treatment. When I see the knot in the process of being untied, it means liberation.

I think about a physical sensation which most of us have experienced — the feeling of a knot in the pit of the stomach. It is a physical response to stress, worry, fear, or frustration which is overwhelming. The return of quiescence does not mean that the knot has disappeared. When we have another encounter involving the same scenario, the question is whether the knot will tighten up again in the wake of the latest emotional turbulence.

In Greek mythology there is a story of Antaeus, who was harassed by Hercules. Each time Antaeus encountered Hercules he would end up in a battered and weakened state. Antaeus learned that he could restore his waning strength simply by letting his body touch the Earth. In order to untie the knot, I must, like Antaeus, come down to earth. I must deal with the reality of my experiences and recognize that no matter how permanent these tendencies appear in my character, I have the ability to begin the process of untying the knot by holding it in balance with its opposite or extreme.

The genesis of a knot in my stomach is the accumulation of the "nots" which I impose upon myself in the outer.

• Alternatively, the twisting here may be for the purpose of uniting the strands into a desirable form.

• The pitcher who twists the ball as he throws it to the batter achieves a curve ball.

• When I dance the twist I stand in one spot and twist my body. The twist was originated by a jolly fellow called Chubby Checker who always smiles when he demonstrates the dance. When I look at this card it can remind me of the dance and I smile.

• Suppose I am wringing a towel or twisting a rope. Where does this take me? Am I doing this for devious reasons? Am I frustrated?

• Twisting someone's arm means that I am working to induce someone to do something. Or, perhaps it is my arm that is being twisted.

• A twister is a drinking spree. Too many twisters will create problems. A twister is also a whirling windstorm, a tornado.

• When I am twisting slowly in the wind, I am being humiliated. It is sort of like being the hanging body on the gallows.

• Twisted may refer to intoxication by narcotics.

• There is a slang expression, "to get one's tit caught in a wringer," meaning someone who gets into a perilous plight or finds themselves to be in a painful situation. Another expression, "I feel like I've been through the wringer," is to have someone give you a hard time. It is an allusion to old fashioned clothes wringers in which clothes are pressed between two rollers to wring out water.

• To have the feeling that you are tied in knots is to feel immobilized or paralyzed by a tangle of mental confusion.

• Another view – to tie the knot is to perform a marriage or to get married.

• To twist someone around my finger means that I exert complete control over another. I can do as I please with this person.

Picture Card 2

This is the symbol of one who has command of the dark forces of the unconscious, a wizard or a witch. They are the physical forms or manifestations of primitive energies; the witch is a projection of the feminine and the wizard is a projection of the masculine. This would also apply to today's fictional super heroes such as Superman and Batman.

This card depicts a figure, its back to the observer. The figure wears a gray cape that hides the torso. Gray is the first color to be perceived. Dreams enshrouded in grayness are from the depths of the unconscious and need to be drawn into the open by a heightened level of consciousness. This card is a signal to me that a working relationship needs to be established with my unconscious. Until now, there has not been enough effort to integrate the messages from the unconscious with the conscious. Left alone the unconscious is undisciplined. My dreams are wild and frightening. I will take a positive approach towards the unconscious. Otherwise its messages will not be assimilated. I am being goaded to become more involved at the level of my unconscious.

• The left arm of the figure is hidden by the cloak, symbolic of the hidden realm of the unconscious. In the picture, the figure reaches high with the right arm toward a golden light, toward intuition, illumination. Right is the direction of heaven. In Ancient Greece, good omens appeared on the right, which symbolized strength, skill, and success. In Western Christian tradition, left denotes the passive and right the active. William of St. Thierry said that the right hand represents knowledge through reason, manifested in works, while the left is wisdom and the contemplative life expressed in peace and silence.

• Red is the dominant color of the card. It is the color of fire and blood and symbolizes the life force and represents strength and power. Feeling and emotion are associated with red. The head of the figure is red and the boots are red. The lining of the cloak appears to be red from the portion of it that shows on the right side of the cloak.

• When I look at the card do I see red? To see red is to become angry, like a bull charging when a red cloth is waved in front of its face.

• Gray is the color that a newborn infant sees and it is the color we see when our eyes are closed. Gray is the center between opposing colors and is a reference point. It is also the Christian symbol of the resurrection of the dead. Medieval artists clothed Christ in a cloak of gray in their paintings of the Last Supper.

• Judging from the portion which is visible, the figure appears to be clad in blue. Blue symbolizes spirit and truth, as in "true blue." The golden light could be energy emanating from the right hand, a "bolt from the blue" or a sudden, unexpected event which alludes to lightning or thunder from a cloudless blue sky. To shoot one's bolt is to do all in one's power, to exhaust resources or capabilities. In archery, a "bolt" is an arrow fired from a crossbow, and to "shoot one's bolt." is to have fired the last of one's supply of arrows. "A fool's bolt is soon shot." Shakespeare *Henry V*, III, vii (1599).

• Blue is used for uniforms, particularly for police. Manual laborers are typically referred to as blue collar workers.

• At my first glance at the cape, I thought it looked like a bell. "Cloak" was the name given to the cape worn by travelers because of its bell shape. "Cloak" was a word literally meaning bell. "Cloak" meaning cape came to have this usage in the thirteenth century. Symbolically, a cloak represents power, separation, concealment, and metamorphosis which relate to how quickly a cloak can change or hide the form. Celtic legends tell of magic cloaks which give the wearer special powers including invisibility and forgetfulness. Cloaks are emblems of royalty, brotherhood, and divine protection.

• Light or fire looks like as if it is being emitted from the hand of the wizard figure on this image card. This is reminiscent of Prometheus, who ridiculed the gods and surpassed everyone in cunning. Prometheus is best remembered for having stolen fire from heaven. For this crime he was chained to a rock on a mountain where a vulture came everyday to eat his liver. The liver grew back everyday for many years. He was freed eventually by Heracles and afterwards gave mankind the fire he had stolen.

• A wizard at his task is considered the top expert in the field.

Picture Card 3

Time does not exist within eternity. By its very nature, eternity is timeless. It has no dimensions and cannot be described with adjectives for to say that it has any characteristic would be to limit it. Time, as we know it, is a fixed, regular, and changeless cycle. Being finite, it cannot exist in eternity.

All motion is circular after it becomes a part of the curve of evolution. Anything circular can be measured and, since time is a circular motion, it can be measured, giving us clocks and calendars. Within eternity there is no conflict. Human beings are in a constant struggle with time, unknowingly yearning for the timelessness of eternity. There is no common ground between time and eternity. St. Augustine described time as the shifting image of motionless eternity.

• When I draw this card it could indicate an attempt to escape from time. An addiction provides temporary relief from the pressures of time, be it sex, alcohol, drugs, or some other ecstasy-escape route. The best temporary escape from time is through meditation. The picture reminds me that I am not a prisoner of time. Time is my milieu. My attempts to escape it are fruitless. One day time will disappear and I will disappear with it. In time I am a being. I have an identity. People know my name. I have characteristics. I belong to a group. When my time ends, I become a non-being.

• Viewed alternatively, when I draw this card it could mean that I am overwhelmed by time, either too much or too little. Or, my attention is being drawn to a particular date and time.

• The calendar reminds me of things or events that are listed or arranged in an orderly way.

• When I want to beat someone's time, it means that I want the affections of another and I have a rival whom I hope to beat out.

• This could mean that I am having a good time or a bad time.

• Doing time means that I feel locked up.

• To be in a time warp means to see things as happening inordinately slow or inordinately fast.

• When I do not care for someone I will not give him the time of day.

• When I am required to do something, this card reminds me that this could be either the perfect time or perhaps long past the right moment.

• This card is about time. Is the card saying that it is about time I performed a long overdue duty?

Picture Card 4

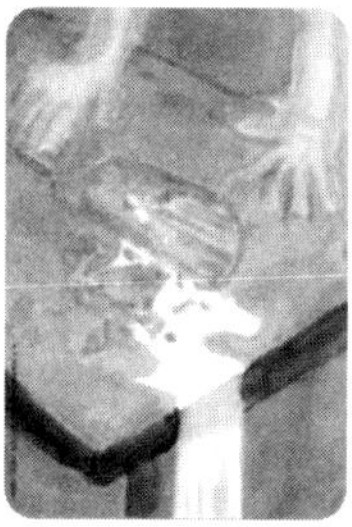

The axiom that one should not cry over spilled milk speaks to plans gone awry, investments gone bad, or unexpected detours brought about by accidental or precipitous movements. The image is one of more than spilled milk. The deeper meaning of this card is about disruption and the potential for physical or emotional injury and ruin.

The glass shards could cause injury if the mess created by the spill is carelessly handled. The hands should be thought of as instruments of accomplishment and action, such as when I say I am going to "set my hands" to a task; this event may interfere and also could have serious consequences. The cow as giver of milk is a symbol of the Mother Earth. With that which has issued forth for my benefit now being wasted I am in danger of loss of supply. This can take several forms: Loss of job, loss of a friendship, or loss of a loved one, or even loss of a pet. The milk has spilled on the table and is also dripping down on the floor and may stain and ruin these surfaces. The image depicts disarray which requires careful attention. The accompanying word card is especially important.

• Alternatively, perhaps my attention is being drawn to the emotion of the moment. Am I surprised? Disgusted?

• I cannot predict how I will react to a loss. This card alerts me to this possibility.

• When I milk something, it means I am trying to take everything out of it.

• When I take money unfairly, I have milked the other for everything I could get.

• The inability to recover spilled milk is a metaphor used throughout history in every culture to signify the futility in trying to undo that which has been done.

Picture Card 5

This card pictures me, male and female, as an accumulation of the many seemingly unconnected, unrelated, *now* experiences of a lifetime. Age means much more than the length of time I have been alive. I see my lifetime as divided into many ages. In the course of seven years or thereabouts every cell of my body has changed. My thoughts today are not those of other ages. My judgments, my emotions, my dreams are also different. I am always under construction, in the process of transformation. Only the name by which I am known remains the same, yet perhaps I would better understand myself if I were to rename myself at every age – like an artist in his blue period or red period.

• My consciousness is in the now, yet my mind is the dwelling place of the multiple now moments of my lifetime, the unconnected recollections of the now moments from childhood to this now. Connections are made, experiences are merged, and meanings are gleaned. "Past," "present," and "future," are on a continuum like a flowing stream.

Through this card I see myself in a now moment, in a Garden of Eden in eternity. The male figure has a newspaper, symbolizing his knowledge of his world. The appearance of the couple is elderly to signify longevity and wisdom. Old age is an appearance. The Taoists say, "Despite your great age, you have the gloss of childhood." An older person who remains spontaneous and inquisitive retains the wonder of youth. The background is green signifying growth and the abode of immortality as in evergreen.

Although these figures are fully clothed, for me the card symbolizes Adam and Eve in the Garden of Eden before the Fall, the state of humankind before human beings became involved with good and evil. Before the pairs of extremes became the standard for earthlings a theoretical paradise existed. I think of the Garden of Eden, without the choices between good and evil, before the instigation of Adam and Eve by the serpent to eat from the forbidden tree of knowledge. Dr. Robert H. Schuller opens each weekly broadcast from the Crystal Cathedral in Garden Grove, California, by saying "This is the Day the Lord has made, let us rejoice, and be glad in it." (*Psalms* 118:24) Each day and each moment are as the moment of God's creation of the first day, before duality.

• *Genesis* 2:18 says, "And the Lord God said 'It is not good that the man should be alone." It is part of human nature to avoid solitude. Blaise Pascal said that learning to be in a room alone is the way to learn to meditate. Fear of being alone is so great that human beings will remain in relationships in which they suffer physical and mental abuse. For this reason, I should consider solitude as an alternative option when considering relationships.

• Viewed alternatively, is the man young and the woman old? What is the state of mind of each of these figures. What emotions do each of them feel? Is there a relationship between them?

• To "age out" means to reach the point in life where you no longer take dope or continue with some other debilitating habit.

Picture Card 6

A social organization is a coming together of solitary persons who lose their individual identity and who become part of a super organism. Everyone in the group is of like mind and strives only for the betterment of the group. Their banner is their rallying point. The writings on the banner express their mantra. Outsiders cannot understand it. The message could be a call to war or a call for spiritual action – their rallying cry. Red in a banner is usually bright since the banner is meant to hearken the members to action. Bright red stands for the masculine energy while dark red stands for the feminine energy. The movement of the banner in the breeze is the breath of the group. Red is the color of fire and blood. This equates with life.

• The card stands for something organized which is based on interdependent activity. For example, the cells of my body fit this description. The card's significance may relate to an auto-immune difficulty. There are other examples: A job situation where each worker depends on the other; an army unit; a religious organization.

• Alternatively, I can view this card as my cheering section, or perhaps as a protest, or maybe it is just my parade.

Picture Card 7

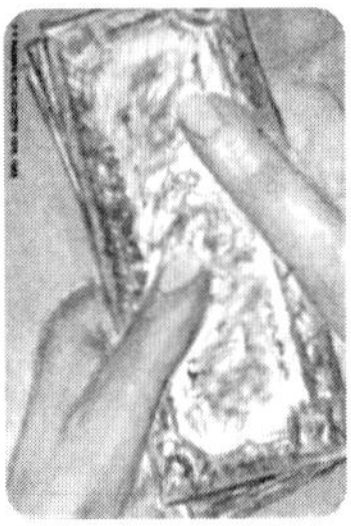

Money represents congealed energy. Congealed energy is spiritual. It cannot be felt or seen. Yet it can accomplish things in the outer. It can see to it that I have a place to rest and food to eat. It can clothe me. This card symbolizes all my effort, my work. The card represents this congealed energy. There are other things I can put in my bank of congealed energy such as good deeds, acts of loving kindness, and living with an emphasis on my own spiritual development. This card asks me to examine my bank of congealed energy.

• In order for the concept of money to be accepted by a general populace, everyone agrees to give worth to the paper on which the money is printed. Paper money is the last step in the movement toward a civilized society. To receive something from another, I can either beg for it or steal it. As groups became more civilized they learned a third way: They could trade for it. The invention of money facilitated the process. Drawing this card could signify my need to take a gentler approach in my business dealings with others. Begging demeans me. Stealing harms others and denigrates me. Learning to use money advances my ability to think in an abstract manner.

• All money is marked with the image of a king, a ruler, a president, or some other leader. It is traditionally seen as a symbol of the soul's image. My soul is marked with the image of its maker.

• Alternatively, I am counting the money I have on hand and I am balancing accounts, or I am rejoicing in how much money I have.

• "Money talks and bullshit walks" means that I should put up or shut up. If I really believe in what I am doing, I am required to sacrifice whatever may be necessary to support it.

• The expression "mony talks," which has found its way into languages the world over, is a metaphor which confers upon money a status so pre-eminent that no other symbolic form approaches it for the emotional intensity displayed by people who seek it or who fight for it. Gamblers ruin their lives over money. Trusted, law-abiding persons suddenly become obsessed with it and embezzle it from their employers. The question posed by this card may bring to mind an obsession I have which has become a major distraction in my normally orderly lifestyle.

• Philanthropy is the reverse of the trait of acquisition. After a person has exhausted the need for acquisition, its opposite sets in: The urge to give to others. Both urges are always present in everyone, except that one or the other usually predominates. When they are in balance, the individual lives harmoniously with the world.

• When I have the ambition and the desire to excel, I am in for a great adventure. I appreciate the things that money can buy. I have the energy to work hard and the energy to play hard. For me the quest for money and success is a game.

• In the 5th Century B.C.E., Euripides wrote that wealth has great influence. In 1532, in *Adagia*, Erasmus wrote about "the talking power of money." This concept has existed since money came into existence.

• The money received by a teacher to promulgate false doctrines is said by Paul to be filthy. (*Titus* 1:11)

Picture Card 8

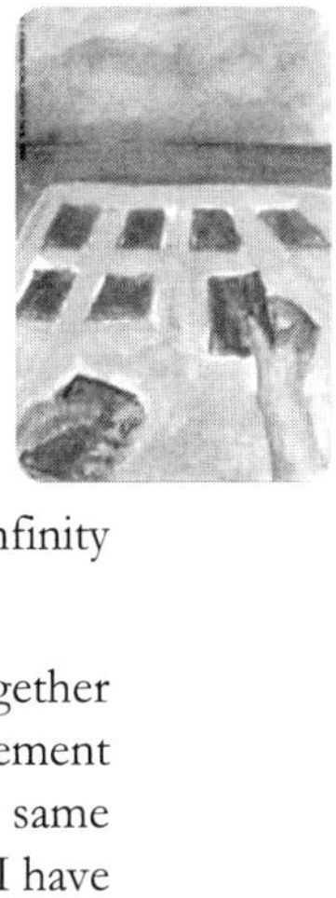

A deck of image cards is a universe of symbols. Examples are the OH Card decks. They become a universe when there is a full deck. Note that the expression "full deck" connotes one who has control of all that is necessary to know. Over the centuries decks of cards became tools for transmitting wisdom about the occult. Their symbols are colors, numbers, elements, people, and words: An infinite array of images! There are 88 image cards and 88 word cards within the two decks of OH Cards. Eight, expressed as an Arabic number, consists of a never-ending double spiral much like the DNA helix. Eight is the number of infinity and the 88 cards constitute the universe of symbols.

The combination of the word cards and the image cards brings together the rational and the mystical. Like the male/female, these two complement each other. They are not opposites. They present two aspects of the same symbol. The card asks me to remember that this is the process in which I have engaged. It asks whether I am committed to the process enough to follow the dictates of the oracle. If my answer is no, I should put away my deck. If my answer is yes, I draw an image card and place it over a word card for further guidance. One of my ambitions is to learn to read the cards and interpret meanings correctly both for myself and for others.

• Alternatively, I am playing a card game which has only one player, such as solitaire. Or I am testing my memory: Can I remember which card is which? Or am I testing my psychic ability? Can I identify the face-down cards without having seen them?

• When someone calls me a card, they mean that I am an eccentric and a remarkable fellow.

• To say that an event is in the cards means that the event is sure to take place.

• When the cards are stacked against me, it means that someone is securing an advantage over me fraudulently.

Picture Card 9

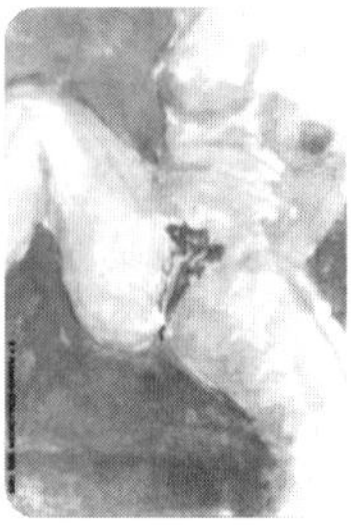

Clothes are to the body as the body is to the soul. When the soul casts off the body as in meditation, it has returned to its original state and is able to claim its divine heritage. Adam and Eve were created in the image of God. They saw the need to put on clothing only after the Fall; their effort to hide themselves means that they had somehow lost that image.

Ezekiel 16:4 uses the metaphor of nakedness to tell the history of Israel. Israel is like a girl who was naked until the Lord chose her and clothed her. Nakedness has the symbol of spiritual purity as well as that of empty sensuality. In this picture the naked female is headless and her arms are not visible, which are other factors for consideration.

The card represents the eternal feminine, the power which draws humankind to transcendency. This is a major cosmic force, the movement towards transcendency coupled with the energy driving us to self-development. The symbolism is reinforced by the color red as the color of the lips of the vagina. Red is the basic symbol of the principle of life. This card asks me to make manifest that which I am hiding. Spiritually I am weak at this moment.

• Viewed alternatively, I can look at the body in biological terms, or I can look at the aesthetic beauty of the feminine form.

• Consider the phrase, "naked truth." It refers to an old fable where Truth and Falsehood go swimming together. Falsehood goes ashore first and puts on Truth's clothing. Truth decides to go naked to avoid wearing Falsehood's garments.

Picture Card 10

The image looks like a dog to me. The Roman Catholic Order of the Dominicans was founded by St. Dominic. The name "Dominicans" derives from two Latin words, *Dominus* which means "Lord" and *canes* which means "dogs" or "hounds." Thus their name "Dominicans" (*Domini-canes*): Hounds of the Lord! The mission of the Dominicans was to combat heresy and defend church dogma through preaching. As Hounds of the Lord, the dogs symbolize Dominicans' faithful service and devotion.

The eyes are riveting, two golden beacons (consciousness) in an otherwise gray and black scenario (unconscious). Eyes are the primary organ of sense perception and symbolically are seen as the window of the soul. They also suggest clairvoyance. Dogs, the faithful companion in life, serve as guides after death through the darkness. Dogs are watchdogs and guard the boundaries between this world and the next.

The right eye stands for the Sun and this corresponds to that which is in motion and expected in the future. The left eye is the Moon and corresponds to that which is at rest and in the past. The card represents the active and the passive energies, both of which are necessary during life and after death. A remote African tribe has a custom they perform at a funeral feast. The dogs are given the dead man's share of the food after these words are spoken, "When you were alive, you yourself could eat. Now that you are dead, your soul eats." The card is asking me to strengthen my soul through prayer, good works, and meditation.

• The card speaks to my paranoia. The figure wears a black watch cape; a ski mask hides the face; the eyes have an animal gleam of reflected light. This person can roam in the dark of night, perhaps to haunt my dreams and awaken me with fright, my heart pounding, my breathing coming in short gasps.

• Alternatively, the card represents a "black" operation, something secret, clandestine, or undercover, an action which may be illegal and for which no accounting is made.

• This image is the dark side, the archetype Jung explained as the shadow.

• Black is the darkness before time began. As a color, black is death and mourning. It conveys the idea of evil and misfortune – black Friday, black market, blackmail, black mass. black magic, blacklist,

• This figure is a black hole. These eyes have sucked up all the light.

Picture Card 11

The focus of this card — through the gaze of the female figure — is upon the child, who stands at ease with hands clasped behind the back. The dress of the woman is dark red, a color symbolizing the centripetal and unifying force which stands for the mystery of life. It is the color of the athanor, the furnace the alchemists used and in which transmutation took place. It was in the athanor that alchemists crafted the Red Stone, the agent of generation and regeneration.

• Carl Jung said that next to God, man is the second creator. God's back symbolizes the cosmic axis, the method by which everything happens. No one sees God face to face. Only God's back is accessible. The woman's hands touch the child's back, the repository of the spine, symbolically the cosmic axis.

• The meaning of this card is affected by the word card and the subject-matter of the reading. It is my inner child and my feminine which are appearing. The currency of this card is the emotion which it stirs within me.

• A child symbolizes innocence. During childhood we are spontaneous. Is she giving the child advice? Is she reprimanding the child? Is she about to embrace the child? Is she going to punish the child?

• The woman (feminine energy) is challenging puerile or infantile attitudes. The woman symbolizes this energy. When she is well integrated in my psyche, I am well adjusted. Here she is with my Inner Child, signifying new growth.

Picture Card 12

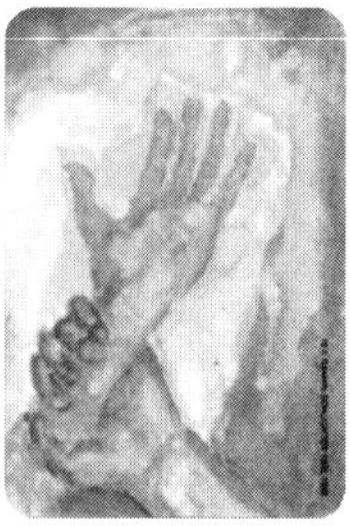

The Latin word for hand is *manus*. From *manus* comes the word "manifestation." That which can be grasped by the hand is said to be manifest. *Psalms* 142:4 says that the right hand represents the place of the elect, heaven. The left hand represents hell.

• The left hand is female, nocturnal, and satanic. The Latin word for left is *sinister*, signaling the ominous, an evil omen. Yin signifies the right and the left is yang. In China the left hand is used for giving and the right hand for taking. The right in politics stands for order and stability while the left stands for those who insist on their rights.

• Yellow is a hot color, the color of great intensity. It speaks of violence and hysteria. Yellow is also the color of deception and cowardice. Red is the color of fire and blood. The card symbolizes how anger begets anger, how violence begets violence.

• The card shows a left hand grasping a left hand. In mathematics two negatives equal a positive. This expresses the axiom that restraint comes out of its likeness or sameness, not out of its opposite.

• Alternatively, I see one hand rescuing the other hand from the flames.

• In politics, order is enforced as much by the left wing as it is by the right wing. Even though I insist on my rights, I am still a supporter of order and stability.

Picture Card 13

Color expresses the principal psychic activities. Red is the color of passion or emotion. Blue is the color of thought. Yellow is the color of intuition. Green is the color of growth. My feelings vary with the tone of colors. Red, orange, and yellow are warm colors. These enhance disputes and antagonism. Singing is primeval. It is innate within the songbird and it also is the same with me. Music is a craft. The card combines mood colors with song and music. This is a symbol of the power of creation and the joy at having been created.

The Ancients attributed the invention of music to Gods or mythical figures: For the Greeks, it was Apollo; the Egyptians, Thoth or Osiris; the Hindus, Brahma; the Hebrews, Jubal. Pythagoras invented a monochord and determined from it a mathematical musical scale. Music for the Pythagoreans is a harmony of numbers which corresponds to a definition of the cosmos. The cosmos can be reduced to sound and numbers. Everything, said Pythagoras, is number. The card invites me to explore my own beginnings, the origins of the universe, and the source of everything in between.

• Once upon a time there were wandering minstrels who sang in order to be fed. Nowadays everyone has to sing for his supper. There is no such thing as a free lunch. Even in the nursery rhyme, "Little Tommy Tucker sings for his supper."

Picture Card 14

The whirling motion is the symbol of evolution, moving from one state to another. Evolution is beyond my control and is controlled by a higher power. The card symbolizes either a downdraft or an updraft, meaning an inevitable and unstoppable process of being sucked down or ejected outward. Evolution is often violent. This results in an abrupt change in my life. I will prepare myself to accept the approaching change.

The motion of the whirl is helicoidal like a tornado. Seen as a cleansing process, as a moving out or eliminating of the old, the helicoidal motion is creative in its nature.

• Viewed as a clockwise motion, the swirl on the card is above the equator and as a counter-clockwise motion, it is below the equator.

• This is a nebulae and signifies new beginnings.

Picture Card 15

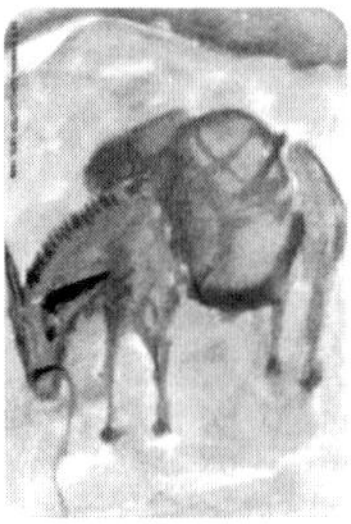

There are many stories of the ass or the donkey. Balaam is on his way to do something he knows he should not do and his she-ass suddenly stops. She can see the invisible angel of the Lord in the road. (*Numbers* 22:23) Abigail loaded asses with food. (*I Samuel* 25:18)

Or there is the story of Joseph putting Jesus and Mary on the back of a she-ass to escape Herod's murderous persecution. An ass was present at the birth of Jesus. The ass is facing an ox. Later on Palm Sunday Jesus makes his triumphant entry into Jerusalem riding a she-ass. (*Matthew* 21:5)

There are diverse symbols involved in each of these stories. With Balaam the donkey is a symbol of patience and courage. At the nativity the donkey is the maleficent facing the beneficent. Later, carrying Jesus into Jerusalem the donkey has been transformed.

The donkey is most often seen as obstinate and stupid, doomed to carry a burden, signifying a person with devilish propensities. The donkey is also seen as symbolizing a person who is bound to the earthly plane of the senses. Remember Pinocchio who abandoned goodness for evil and wound up with the ears of a donkey. The question: Am I making an ass of myself?

This image asks me to reconsider my obstinacy, to learn patience, and always to carry my share of the load. The ass, its head lowered, stands still. The setting is a desert. Symbolic of the world deprived of God, the desert is barrenness. With God, it is fruitfulness. It invites me to pause to examine my spiritual health. The desert is a place of abandonment and desolation. The desert also represents peace and contemplation. The children of Israel sojourned there for 40 years and Christ was tempted in the desert where he spent 40 days.

Picture Card 16

A checkerboard is a pattern of geometrical shapes, usually squares. We play the games of checkers or chess on these boards. The checkerboard itself is a symbol of the visible world. Usually the board is done in contrasting colors such as black and white and this symbolizes the light and the darkness which together entwine the world. Each square segues into its opposite such as yin following yang. There are 64 squares on the checkerboard, the same as the number of hexagrams in the *I*

Ching. Sixty-four is the number which signifies cosmic unity. It is the square of eight and represents earthly wholeness and fulfillment. Traditionally Jesus belongs to the sixty-fourth generation from Adam.

•The checkerboard also may be a symbol for a battleground, for example, a competition between that which is rational versus the instinctive or that which is ordered and predetermined versus that which occurs by chance.

• The box is the feminine symbol of the unconscious. There is always a secret within the box. Except that this box is open. I let my mind do a flip and the black bottom of the box becomes the top of a different structure. The colors of the board are green and gold. Green is a combination of blue and yellow. It vacillates between hot and cold. Gold is the perfect metal. Each corner of the box is a gold square.

• The counterpart of Eve in Greek mythology is Pandora. Her husband, Epinetheus, had been given a box by Zeus which contained all the ills of the world. Pandora ignored her husband's order not to open the box and from that day forward the world has had its problems. Like the sameness of the squares on the board, events repeat themselves over and over. When we see them repeating, we invent stories of how things came to be the way they are. Difficult childbirth for women preceded the stories of Eve and Pandora. We invent stories and metaphors in order to create ideas about groups. Both stories, that of Eve and of Pandora, are designed to promote the idea that women were somehow responsible for the world's problems.

• The Greek word for box, *pyxis*, was also the word used for a woman's vagina. This gives added significance to the obvious prejudice of the author of the Pandora story. Seen from this perspective, the card asks me to examine my attitude toward a group I view as inferior or jinxed.

• Alternatively, I see a puzzle: Is this an anagram, checkerboard, a box, the squares? Is it breakfast cereal, a throwback to my childhood?

• Whenever I encounter a symbol either awake or in a dream, I let my conscious mind do a transit into the unconscious and allow whatever wants to come forth to surface. The squares on a checkerboard are constantly alternating, much like the movement from one extreme to another. For example, when I have vacillated between good and evil I am said to have had a checkered past. It applies also to a person who moves from job to job.

• More examples: The checkerboard could bring to mind the words "pick up the check" (do I need to examine my stinginess?); or, "get a checkup" (do I need to see a doctor?); or, a reality check (am I living in a dream world?).

Picture Card 17

I compare this card with Picture Card 69, the two figures. What differences do I note? None of the five figures is moving or walking. Or are they on a magic carpet which transports them past life's experiences and events? I look at the picture and let my mind turn around until another image appears.

Three is fundamental in the cosmos. The Chinese saw three as a perfect number, representative of heaven, expressive of wholeness. I think of the three wise men, the triangle, the Trinity, the "om" which is the sound of the three letters "A," "U," "M," (AUM) which match the three states of manifestation. I think of three cheers, three strikes, things happening in three's, the many godheads which appear in three's. I look at the colors they wear: two reds, two blues, a green, and a brown. Are these people related? I look at their hair. What is the object on the left?

• Alternatively, two people from outer space have come to take me away. Or perhaps I am just ambling along with friends. Is the threesome a family?

Picture Card 18

The symbol of moving up a stairway signifies the ascent to knowledge of the divine world. Moving down a stairway signifies a movement to knowledge of the unconscious. The stairway is gray, a color which is a mixture of black and white. A white stairway means higher knowledge. A black stairway signifies black magic. Gray is the color of the Christian symbol for the resurrection of the dead. Jesus is wearing a gray cloak in medieval portraits of the Last Judgment. Ashes and mists are gray. Ancient Hebrews introduced the practice of putting ashes on their heads to demonstrate grief. When the weather is misty people get depressed.

At the top of the stairway (or is it at the bottom of the stairway ?) there is an open door through which a yellow light can be seen. Yellow is the hottest of all the colors, like molten steam flowing from a furnace. I think of the yellow Sun searing through the blue of the sky. Yellow is also the color of gold. I notice that there is no such thing as dark yellow since yellow is such a bright color. After his ascent to heaven, Jesus is pictured with a yellow halo. Yellow announces approaching death. It is the color of jealousy, deception, and adultery. Yellow paint on a warrior's face indicates cruelty. The ambivalence of yellow is best demonstrated in Islam where golden yellow means wisdom and pale yellow means treachery.

The door signifies a passing from one stage to another. With this card I know that I am moving from the known into the unknown, from the profane to the sacred. When this card appears I examine each of the symbols. It is a card of deep symbolic significance.

• Like the false door in the tombs of ancient Egypt, the doorway is a passageway to come and go from one realm to another. Am I making a transition? Am I looking for a way to return to former experiences?

• A closed door symbolizes a shutting out of someone or something in your life. An open door symbolizes that you have an expectant attitude, that you would welcome newness in the form of a new friend or relationship or a new project.

• Gray means neither black nor white. It is not a mixture of the two. Black remains black and white remains white. Their coming together creates a third area. For instance when a matter is between legality and illegality, it is said to be in the gray area.

Picture Card 19

Green is a color of mystery. It symbolizes the hidden knowledge of nature and of fate. It is a combination of the blue and the yellow. Unlike yellow, blue rarely occurs in nature. When I see a blue sky I am really looking at a void. Green appears midway between the blue of the heavens and the yellow-red of hellfire. It predominates on earth where it is the color of plant life and associated with the life cycle. Green is the blossoming of life and is the color of immortality. It is a female color.

• If different cultural groups had colors, green would be the color of the middle class. In the Middle Ages, physicians wore green. Green is a common color of the scrub suits of surgeons and their staffs in the United States. Also in the United States, green is the color of money.

Christianity evolved in temperate climates where water and greenery abound. Islam prospered in the land of deserts, where mirages are common. Yet the flag of Islam is green and green is the symbol for Muslims. The Prophet's cloak was green. Medieval painters depicted the cross of Jesus as green. The Cross represents the regeneration of humankind through the sacrifice of Jesus Christ.

In ancient Egypt cats with green eyes were greatly feared. Anyone who killed such a cat was executed. Alchemists teach that the light of the emerald pierces all secrets. Green is the color of the buds of spring and the color of slime and gangrene. Thus there is a green of life and a green of death. Yet green remains the most tranquil of all colors; it knows neither joy nor sadness. All symbols carry a life force since they open doors to reflection and ideas. Yet they are coded and must be deciphered. Green is a fine example of the expression of a symbol.

• The bedroom is the symbol of regeneration: Sleep, sex, birth, and death. Ceremonies around birth, marriage, and death are the rituals most related to the mysteries of life. The bed is like the earth: It gives life and it receives life. In the New Testament when Jesus healed the man who was paralyzed he told him to take up his bed and walk. (*Matthew* 9:5) The bed symbolized the body of the sinner which had been cleansed and restored by grace. Read also *Genesis* 48:2 and 49:33, the story of how Jacob symbolically uses his bed in the ritual of death.

• There are three mysteries in this card: The mystery of rejuvenation, which has to do with illness and disease; the mystery of magnetism, which has to do with how people are drawn to each other; and the mystery of transition, which has to do with moving from life on this plane to the next plane. I choose the mystery which suits me at this moment.

• Alternatively, this is the bedroom of a couple. Are they newlyweds or old people? There are two pairs of slippers. The figurines next to the lamp conjure up other images.

• A person who is green is considered a beginner and new at whatever is transpiring. Does this apply to me? Am I green with envy about something?

• In *Othello* (3:3), Shakespeare tells the story of the green-eyed monster who toys with its prey before eating it. Undoubtedly he was referring to a cat with a mouse. Today the green-eyed monster takes possession of a person and turns him jealous. The green in the drawing could signify the rise of jealousy in me.

• Shakespeare also used the color green in *Cleopatra* (3:2) in describing the desire for another's possessions. He called envy the green sickness.

• A person who is nauseated is said to be green around the gills.

Picture Card 20

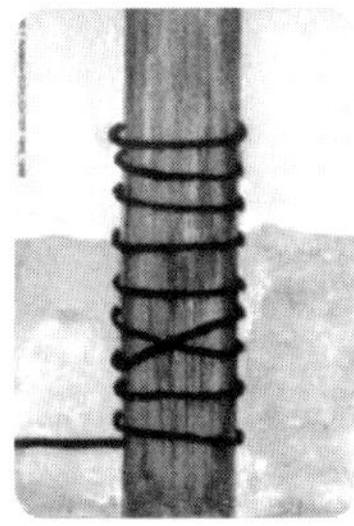

Each time I draw a picture card I put myself directly into the picture itself. I see myself in this card entwined with a girdle. My arms are free while my body is laced to the wooden pillar.

• The deep significance of this card is standing fast. In Celtic tradition the story is told of Cùchulainn, a mighty warrior. Legend has it that he was so good with a sword that he could cut the grass under your feet and the only thing you would notice would be the grass falling. He could shave you and you would never notice it.

The stories of Cùchulainn accomplish the same thing: The symbolism gains a universality and an eternality. He had himself bound to a pole so that he would die on his feet during the battle. "The Cattle Raid of Cooley" tells the story of how Cùchulainn cut off the heads of twelve enemy soldiers and set each on the top of a pillar. After his own death a fellow warrior avenged Cùchulainn's death by killing his murderer, Lugaid, and setting his head upon a pillar. The pole in the card signifies stability in me, the strength of my personal character. I may pull the pole down by my misdeeds, much like Samson, or I may gird myself and stand tall like Cùchulainn.

• When an actual event is taken and symbolic interpretation is drawn from it, it gives the event an added dimension. The event moves beyond time and space. An example: Cool Papa Bell, a baseball player from the old Negro Leagues was said to be so fast that he could flip the switch turning out the lights and be under the covers before the lights went out. Here the symbolic interpretation builds the legend of how fast Cool Papa was on the bases.

• Alternatively, this card is the representation of the world axis, the point of unity of mind and matter.

Picture Card 21

• Alchemy is the art of transmutation. Early and persistent efforts of alchemists went into attempting to change base metals into gold. The Chinese alchemists even produced a golden elixir meant to prolong physical life. Jade was considered to be magical. It was melted down and mixed with mercury as a potion which would give the drinker eternal life. It seems naive to us that learned scholars in past centuries put so much thought and effort into what seems impossible to us.

The assumption is that alchemists are the forerunners of today's chemists. This is untrue. Alchemy is a symbolic activity. Gold represents immortality. For an alchemist the ultimate transmutation is transforming me into an immortal. When I achieve Godhead, when God and I are indistinguishable, the transmutation is complete.

• When the symbols of fire and water come together, a spark of creativity comes about. Alcohol is the material substance produced when symbolic fire and symbolic water synthesize. Native Americans intuitively called it firewater: It disappears along with that which it burns. In its material form, alcohol stimulates that which is latent within the drinker and creates a whole new language and a different (up until now, hidden) way of thinking. Everything, of course, carries its opposite effect as well and alcohol is no different. In addition to its spark of creativity and stimulation of thought, it also brings about forgetfulness and death.

Movie plots provide examples. The drinkers Nick and Nora Charles in the "Thin Man" series drink constantly but remain witty and are able to solve complex crimes. In contrast, "The Lost Weekend" and "Days of Wine and Roses" are portrayals of the devastating effects of alcoholism with its blackouts and episodic *delirium tremens.*

This ambivalence of alcohol reminds me of its alchemical origin: Alcohol flaming up with the masculine symbol of fire, lighting up the world, and submerging the drinker into oblivion with the feminine symbol of water.

•Symbols of alchemy are frequently an aspect of fairy tales or myths. For example, in the fairy tale of Snow White and the Seven Dwarfs an alchemist would say that Snow White is a virgin who is seeking gold. Dwarfs are also called gnomes, a word which derives from *gnosis*, a Greek word which means knowledge. There are seven metals. Each dwarf takes on the character of the planet which governs him. Dopey represents the Moon. The word *lunar* gives us "lunatic" or more appropriately the colloquialism, "looney," which describes Dopey. Grumpy is saturnine, reflecting a coldness and a detachment. He represents the melancholy of Saturn. Venus is pleasant and thus the Dwarf, Happy. Doc, the leader, is the Sun. Mercury being passive in alchemical terms is Bashful, Jupiter is Sleepy and Mars is Sneezie.

In the end it is the melancholic Grumpy who always comes up with the right answers. Snow White is to be put to death by the Green Hunter. Green means regeneration. Symbolically, hunting is a spiritual quest for the divine. A golden apple is the symbol of immortality. This one though contains poison and Snow White appears to die after eating the apple. Mercury is the symbol of eternal youth and Prince Charming represents Mercury. Snow White marries Prince Charming and they live happily ever after.

• The drinker in the card is alone and at a bar. To be alone because I want solitude and introspection is to seek a oneness within myself. However when I have the sense that I am alone in a public place of assembly, I am dealing with fear, a lack of trust, and loneliness.

A bar is an obstruction. The bar signifies an inner blockage, the inability to pierce the wall of self-doubt to reach the goal of self-understanding. Excessive drinkers ask "why?" incessantly. "Why" asks for a lie. No answers are forthcoming until there is a sense of powerlessness. There is a bar within me. Rather than remove it, perhaps it can be harmonized with openness.

• When I draw this card my immediate response is to look for obstructions which I have built within myself. Next I begin the process of transmutation through meditation. For me, questions are answered in the silence.

• Alternatively, suppose this is a restaurant instead of a bar. Suppose also that one man is eating while the other is ordering from the menu. I can now interpret the card according to my need for nourishment.

• Letting my mind do a turnaround, the card represents a bar of music. Ballet dancers practice on a bar. When admitted to practice law, an attorney has passed the bar. In the Army, the rank of First Lieutenant is a silver bar, a Second Lieutenant, a gold bar; and a Captain, two gold bars. A slot machine gambler looks forward to the triple bar.

• Before streets were paved, water wagons drawn by horses sprayed the roads to keep down the dust. Today's expression signifying abstinence from booze, "on the wagon," is a reference to that water wagon of bygone years.

Picture Card 22

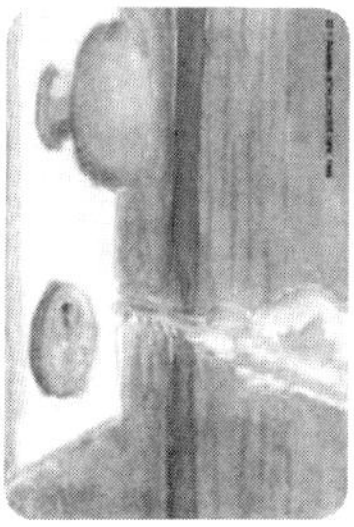

A key has dual symbolism. Since it can either lock or unlock a door, it symbolizes opening up or closing down. When I have found the secret of a particular mystery, it means that I have been initiated into a spiritual state or moved to a higher level. Absence of the key means that I am shut out of such esoteric knowledge.

• Peter symbolically received the keys to the kingdom of heaven from Jesus and was able thereby to open or to close the heavenly gates. Each successive Pope has used the symbol of the two keys to indicate his divine power. The two keys are emblazoned on the papal coat of arms, one silver and one gold.

Before there were Popes, the symbol of two keys belonged to the Roman God, Janus. These keys opened the gates of the two solstices, starting the waxing and waning cycles of the year, summer and winter. Janus is pictured with two faces, one looking in each direction.

• I have access to a key to my own spirituality. Using it to lock or unlock my personal mystery is my individual decision. The door in the picture signifies the passage from one world to another, from the known to the unknown, even a passage from the light (conscious) to the darkness (unconscious).

• In fairy tales there are usually three keys, each opening a different door to a new mystery. The key symbolizes a riddle which has to be solved or a mystery to be understood.

• Putting my valuables under lock and key means that they are securely stored.

Picture Card 23

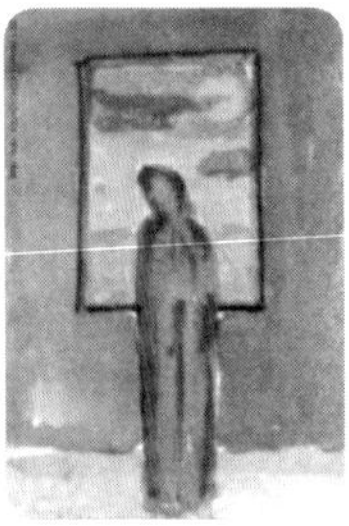

When I cover my head and my body with a hooded cloak, I have done more than make myself invisible. Monks and nuns who don such attire do so to symbolize their withdrawal from the world and dedication to God. This is a surrender of identity.

The card is about my need to drop all sense of my personal self and to dwell in the spirit. The steps I take to accomplish this are to master entry into my unconscious through deeper study and interpretation of my dreams and frequent use of my OH Cards. There is a certain nostalgia about saying farewell to myself. In bidding this fond goodbye I open myself to a process which will lead me to my patterning and to my unique identity.

• Cloaks are worn as marks of authority as in the case of a monarch or a magistrate. Official acts are done under the cloak of authority. In academia, the cloak or robe is a symbol of acquired wisdom.

• Alternatively, this is a statue in front of a painting. I move closer to the statue in order to determine the identity of the sculptured piece and to learn more about the painting.

• The figure has a ghostly appearance. The features of the face are not discernible. That which is behind the figure is another dimension, a different world. The clouds are moving in front of the Sun and the darkness of the clouds is fading because of the Sun's brilliance.

• The cloak is not a cape. Rather, a cape is identified with the world's axis. For example, a priest robed in a chasuble or cape is ritually at the center of the universe. The priest becomes the dwelling place of God, whose representative he is.

Picture Card 24

The shepherd is a symbol of the leader of his people. The flock belongs to God and the shepherd has been chosen by God to guide the flock and be its protector and provider. The shepherd has an intuitive wisdom and symbolizes watchfulness, experience, and loving care. The best known expression of the symbolism of shepherd is *Psalms* 23. Herds of animals must be cared for and encouraged to multiply. Like horticulture, taking care of flocks or herds is a feminine function.

• The symbol of the shepherd is that of one who has a sense of wisdom which is born of experience and who also is intuitive. The shepherd means one who is alert, watchful and vigilant. The shepherd is always awake, always keeping an eye on everything. The shepherd always knows where to find pastures for the flock to graze and which are the safe streams for them to drink water. The opposite of the shepherd/herdsman is the farmer. The shepherd is always on the move; the farmer stands still. It is action versus passivity.

• There is a Welsh tale about two flocks of sheep, one white and one black. A river runs between them. Whenever a white sheep bleats, a black sheep crosses the river and turns white. Whenever a black sheep bleats, a white sheep crosses the river and becomes black. Next to the river there is a very tall tree. Half of the tree is in flames; half is filled with leaves. Like the angels ascending and descending Jacob's Ladder, the sheep represent souls descending from heaven to Earth and ascending from Earth to heaven.

• Caesar wrote that the gods require a life in return for a life. The sudden population boom the world is experiencing would be balanced by the millions of people killed as a result of war, starvation, epidemics, accidents, genocide, homicide, and natural disasters, according to this theory. Pythagoras expressed the same belief and called it *metempsychosis*, the transmigration of souls.

• In this card the shepherd, like Moses, is the conductor moving the sheep from one reality to another. When interpreting this card I look to the duality of the situation or to the scenario of the question.

• In *Matthew* 25:32, Jesus predicted that in the afterlife, the sheep would sit on God's right-hand and the goats on the left, drawing a distinction between the compliant and the resistant.

Picture Card 25

The female breast is a symbol of protection. The infant is placed just above the heart whose rhythm has comforted the baby while it was in the womb. At the nipple is found nourishment, giving the card the triple symbol of security, plenty, and comfort.

• Yet the breast has a deeper symbolization. In Hebrew the word *bat* means daughter and measurement of liquid. The Hebrew word *emah* means mother and measurement. The connection between mother/daughter and measure is this: The mother/daughter represents the feminine principle; measure means limitation since anything which can be measured has limitation. On the other hand the male principle cannot be measured; it is limitless.

The deeper meaning of the female breast as a symbol is rooted in its function as supplier of milk. Milk is the first food and the first drink. A dream of milk references eternal truths. The breast is something finite performing a function of infinity. The female breast takes on sexual symbolization when it is concealed and then revealed in a ritual flirtation or dance. The limited feminine principle attracts the male principle joining the finite and the infinite.

• In ancient times, a couple which produced no children was held in low esteem. It was considered a disgrace. The people of those times believed that every event, especially one like childbirth, was ordained by a Divine Being. There were no such things as natural phenomena. Everything from tornadoes to snowfalls could be attributed to a Divine Agency.

• There are three ways of seeing events: As events brought about by a "God" who is external to me, as events brought about by a "God" which dwells within me, or as events which occur naturally and God is not the explanation.

• This card asks me to suggest a mode of thinking which is uniquely mine.

• A bared breast is an act of supplication; beating the breast is repentance.

• The human breast has been long considered the place of sentimental feelings and secrets. Thus, when I say I will make a clean breast of something, it means that I will open my heart and tell all.

Picture Card 26

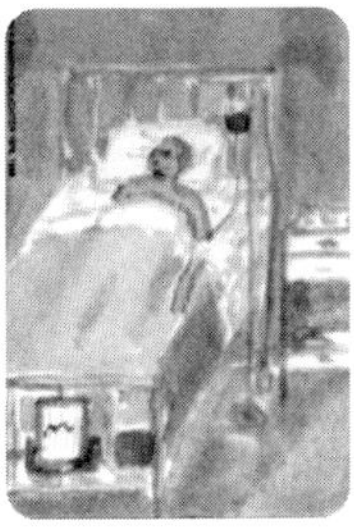

An oath is the symbol of an agreement with a human or with a divine being. The covenant is actually with the entire cosmos which the oath-taker calls upon as surety for the pledge. When you pledge your word you place it in the patterned order of things. You take responsibility for breaking up that order if your word is broken.

The blood in the card hangs from a pole which represents the axis around which the patient's life rotates. The seven bars on the bed represent Heaven (3) and Earth (4), the fullness of the universe in motion. While the bed is also the symbol of love and sleep, here it represents the place of death. Yet the life-force is transforming the patient. The chart tells the story of this effort.

• When I receive this card I realize that I am undergoing a regeneration process. Assistance is available from an unknown source. There is every promise of progress. I understand that the order of things is disrupted whenever there is a broken promise. Seriousness of the matter is emphasized by the presence of the pole, representing the cosmic ordering of events. When I alter events I do battle with the cosmos itself.

• Oath-taking came into existence before recorded history began. No wonder then that oath-taking has for millennia been associated with blood. Blood symbolizes life itself. It also represents fire and heat, attributes of the Sun.

The Roman Catholic doctrine of transubstantiation is based on the same symbolic oath. In order to preserve the blood-sharing practice for all time, Jesus promises his disciples that the wine they consecrate will be His Blood and that it will afford them and their successors eternal life. Ancient tribes drew blood from the limbs of initiates and mixed it with that of the other members, thus achieving absolute consanguinity. The custom has been and is worldwide. Witness the practice of Native Americans making blood-brothers or the Knights Templar who each put drops of their blood in a chalice with wine which everyone then drank. The custom crosses cultures. Chinese brides and grooms to this day still exchange blood.

• The practice of taking an oath on a sacred object dates to the 10th century. Eventually, in some cultures the Bible came to be that object. When I say that I will swear on a stack of Bibles, does this mean that what I will say is more likely to be truthful than not?

Use of caverns as sites of mystery training goes back in recorded history at least to Zoroaster. Porphyry writes that:

"Zoroaster was the first to dedicate a natural grotto watered by springs and thick with foliage and flowers, to Mithras. This cave represented the shape of the world which Mithras had created. . . . Inspired by these beliefs, the Pythagoreans, and after them, Plato, called the world a cavern or grotto. In fact, according to Empedocles, the powers which guide souls say, 'We have come into this grotto covered by a roof.'" Porphyry, Concerning the Nymphs' Grotto, 6-9

• Most secret cults or societies have a death-imitation ritual for new members. This usually meant placing the candidate in a cavern or a pit, a symbolic return to the womb. The story of Jesus and Lazarus illustrates the use of the cavern in antiquity for ritualistic purposes.

Jesus was a spiritual guru with a substantial following. His small inner circle consisted of twelve men. The next level was made up of seventy-two men whose function was to form groups or churches in distant cities. These men participated in secret rituals and initiatory practices. Lazarus was one such initiate. Apparently Jesus was late arriving at the initiation ceremony and Lazarus was left bound in the cavern for three days. There was danger that Lazarus really had died. When Jesus called him forth and he emerged unscathed, a myth arose that Lazarus had risen from the dead.

Jesus was born in a cave, which was in a rock-cut stable. After the crucifixion, Jesus was laid to rest in a tomb carved out of rock. To enter a cavern is to return to your beginning and then to reunite with the Deity. Christians believe that the Light of Redemption and the Word shone out from the stable. The cavern also represents the womb which explains why so many mystery religions require initiates to enter a cavern or why Jesus' born again requirement involved the death-imitation ritual.

• Pythagoras dwelled in a cavern when he initiated his life and transformed himself. In Chinese the same ideogram, *tong*, stands for cavern as well as for penetration. Therefore I understand that when I draw this card I must look within myself for the Cavern of Eternity. Plato called the cavern a place of ignorance, suffering and punishment in which human beings were chained and imprisoned by the Gods. (*Republic*, 7:514 a, b)

• There once was a man in antiquity named Trophonius who had achieved a reputation as an architect of note. He and his brother, Agamedes, built the Temple of Apollo at Delphi, home of the most famous oracle in the history of the world. Later, King Hyrieus commissioned the brothers to build his treasury. Trophonius was himself the ruler of a petty kingdom. He and his brother were well-situated but they did not possess great wealth. They decided to dig a secret passage to the treasury while they were building it so that they could later steal the king's treasure. Hyrieus became suspicious of such a plot and set a trap. After the treasury building was completed and the king's treasure was securely stored, Trophonius and Agamedes entered the treasury one night through the secret passageway. Unaware of the trap, Agamedes made a false move and was ensnared in chains. Trophonius tried desperately to free him and could not. He was so anxious that his thefts not be discovered and knowing that if his brother were discovered he himself would be incriminated, he cut off his brother's head, tucked it under his arm, picked up a bag of gold, and turned to leave. Just then the earth opened up and Trophonius was swallowed into the bowels of the earth.

• Many years later there happened to be a drought. The Delphic Oracle was consulted. The priestess directed them to a cavern deep in a virgin woods. She told the people that Trophonius dwelled in the cavern. The cave of Trophonius thereafter became the oracle which one consulted when inquiring about frightening experiences. A series of deep underground passageways lead to the cavern's entrance, which opens to a cold and yawning chasm. There is no light. To reach it, there is a climb down a ladder into another chasm with a very narrow entrance which must be entered feet first with a drop of about eight feet to the floor below. A stay in the cavern's interior lasts up to 24 hours. On emerging from the cavern, frightening experiences are recalled while seated in the Chair of Memory. Traditionally during this era whenever one encountered a sad and serious person it was said that that person must have consulted the Oracle of Trophonius.

• Finally, the cave represents the unconscious, more particularly the shadow or dark material, the unexpected and frightening experiences which manifest in everyone's dreams and experiences. When I deny the truth of my past in order to suppress my feelings of guilt, I am said to have a Trophonius Complex. The shadow is a process. I create it by making symbols of the material which I suppress or to which I deny expression. When I give this material full expression, I unleash my power source. The past though is so thoroughly a part of my psyche that it cannot be erased except for loss through brain injury. Short of this, the first step is to accept the past as my own. I acknowledge it. Carlos Castenada says I should leap into it. I embrace it. I recognize it in the light, out of the shadow.

• The symbolization of the card is that the cavern is my primal ego swallowed up in the bowels of my unconscious. No matter if I am a Trophonius or a Cain, I have a stain or blot seeking exposure to my conscious self. Within the cavern is my reservoir of energy which will free me when I enter and liberate myself. This is the brilliance of the Swiss psychiatrist Rorschach in creating shapeless ink blots which become symbols for the individual performing much the same function as the cavern.

• The cat in the card is the strict guardian of my unconscious. It stands as a stark reminder of the evil and diabolical hang-ups I will discover when I enter the cavern. Buddhists believe that cats and snakes were the only creatures unmoved by the death of Buddha. Similarly the Kabbalah sees the cat and the serpent as representing the misuse of the good things of life. Once I enter the cavern of the unconscious I learn that the cat is really pleasant. I also discover that it is the cat's higher wisdom which allows the cat to disdain emotion over death and to take advantage of the good which presents itself.

• Occasionally the earthen walls of a cave will collapse or "cave in." Metaphorically speaking, I cannot ever cave in. I remain steadfast.

In *Piers Ploughman*, William Langland retells the Aesop fable about the mice who decide to put a bell around the neck of the cat so that they could be alerted when the cat came around. The idea was great one, since it would undoubtedly save a great many lives. The problem was that finding a mouse who could bell the cat proved to be an impossible task. The card reminds me to think through my ideas before I put them into practice.

Picture Card 28

The Chinese use the same ideogram for the words *flag* and *being*. The flag literally stands for a person. A description of the flag calls forth the genius and bravery of the leader. The flag is alive. Its emblem speaks of the spirit and the qualities of a group's ability to defend itself and to protect itself against evil forces. *Exodus* 17:15 says *Jehovah nissi*, the Lord is my flag. All religious groups have flags just as do all nations.

• The insignia on the flag of a nation, state, or organization gives the group its psychic energy. In the card the soldiers are marching in step, signifying readiness. The throng is anonymous, signifying compliance. In battle, the flag identifies the command. It is protected from capture. It was a high honor for a soldier in the Civil War to be chosen to bear the colors of his fighting unit and stand in the midst of the fighting. If the flag bearer was wounded and the flag went down, another soldier would rush in to hold it high. The flag is protected at all costs. After a furious battle, a Union company was distressed because it was thought that its flag had been captured. The colors bearer was killed but apparently in the fury of the battle he had saved the flag from capture by hiding it inside his tunic. He died a hero. To honor the flag is to honor the nation and to honor oneself. It is an emotional symbol that can stir a people to serve and to die for a cause.

• This card calls upon me to raise an emblem of own. I must determine what it represents about me. My flag changes according to my mood and is affected by activities around me. If I am balanced I might draw a flag which depicts music, say a musical scale. If I am out of balance, my flag will portray turmoil, perhaps a storm. My standards are my flag. Creating my own flag, complete with colors, is a wonderful ritual.

Picture Card 29

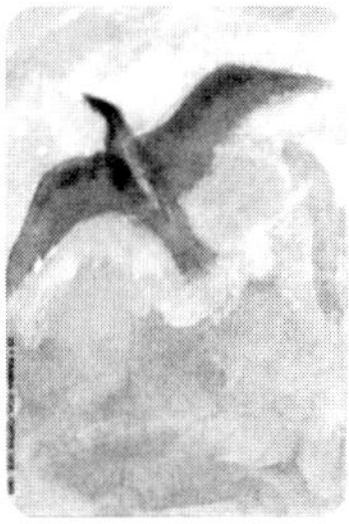

Because of their connection to the sky, birds are an ancient symbol as mediators between Heaven and Earth. Although in some cultures, particular birds such as ravens and vultures are seen as an evil omen, birds are generally perceived as auspicious, representing goodness and joy. The bald or white-headed eagle is the emblematic Bird of Freedom of the United States. The "blue bird of happiness" of song and poem originated as a visionary concept from a play produced in 1910 about a boy and girl seeking "the blue bird" of happiness. Throughout the world there is a legend that storks bring newly born babies. People in Germany even put up storks outside their homes to announce a birth.

• When angels are imaged, they are given wings to signify that they are transmitters of divine messages. Some beliefs teach that after death the soul departs from the body as a bird. In Egypt this was depicted by *Ra*, a human-headed hawk. Birds figure in creation myths and as forces in control of the elements, *e.g.*, the Native American Thunderbird and the Lightning Bird of southern Africa. The Mesoamerican snake-bird Quetzalcoatl has both celestial and earthly powers.

• Particular birds symbolize particular ideas. The dove is the symbol of peace, tenderness, innocence, and love. In Christian art, the Holy Ghost is symbolized in the form of a dove and the seven rays proceeding from it are the "Seven Gifts of the Spirit." The dove symbolizes deliverance from anxiety. When the dove returned to Noah with a twig he no longer worried about whether he would ever find land. (*Genesis* 8:8-12) The dove also typifies innocence.

• The stork is sacred in Sweden based upon the legend that it flew around the cross crying "Strengthen, strengthen." The robin redbreast is said to have picked a thorn out of Jesus' crown on his way to Calvary. A drop of blood fell on the bird and dyed its breast red.

• It is written that "he who understands has wings." This means that my intellect is swifter than the flight of birds. Wings express a spiritual desire, a release from the ego which unites the mundane with the purifying air of love and ecstasy. I am freed from gravity, approaching an orgasm of my spirit. I want to move to something higher than my earthbound human state.

• Those of us in Nature who need large eyes or wide eyes have them. The eye of the eagle is nearly as large as the elephant's eye.

Picture Card 30

The ideogram for yin and the ideogram for yang both have the word Fu contained within them. Fu means a hill or a slope. Yin means dull or gloomy weather with overcast skies. Yang denotes the Sun, rising over the horizon. The yin ideogram and the yang ideogram describe two sides of a valley, one bathed in sunlight and the other shrouded in shadow. Yin and yang symbolize the rhythm of the world, a bright side and a dark side, positive and negative, male and female, all the pairs of extremes.

The nature of the cosmos is that it is complementary. Everything contains its opposite. In the I Ching, yin is expressed by a broken line, while yang is expressed by a straight line. The symbol of yin-yang is a circle divided into equal halves by a wavy line. The yang half is white and the yin half is black. The length of the dividing line equals half of the circle's circumference. The total perimeter of each half equals the total circumference of the circle. The yin half has a yang dot and the yang half has a yin dot symbolizing their interdependence.

• For Tibetan Buddhists, blue is the color of *vairocana*, which symbolizes transcendent wisdom and one's potential. It also speaks of emptiness as of a blue sky. For Tibetan Buddhists blue symbolizes the primordial conscience, the law which governs all. It is omnipotent and it is this law *(dharmadh~tu)* which opens the door of liberation. Blue is the color of the yang. It also represents the dragon and therefore is beneficent. Green is the color of thunder in the I Ching. It corresponds to the trigram ch'eu, the Arousing, the beginning of the rise of the yang. It is the color of immortality. The yellow in the card represents the midday Sun. Yellow is also the color of fertile soil. In ancient China couples about to marry are advised to have yellow sheets and pillows to assure a fully harmonized yin and yang.

• Put simply, to be fully harmonized with yin and yang means my being in the right place at the right time, a perfect alignment of events with time and space.

• An arch has mystical qualities. It serves as a support of the weight above it by resolving vertical pressure into what is called horizontal thrust. The significance of the use of an arch above the yin-yang symbol tells me the yin-yang principles are based upon mysticism.

Picture Card 31

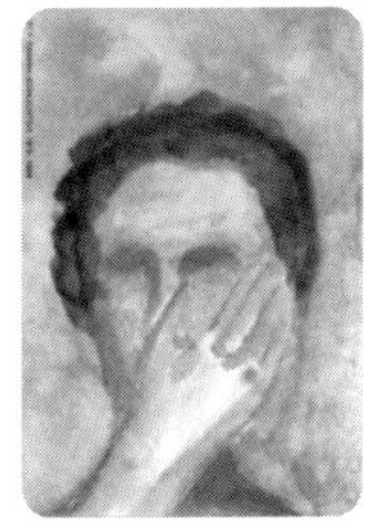

My face was not made for me. It is for the benefit of others. I cannot see my face directly. It is constantly sending a message about my inner self – whether I am happy, sad, angry, peaceful, or any one of a myriad of emotions. There is no part of the body more important. All my sense organs are in my face.

• The Hebrew word for face, *panim*, is plural, which is significant because the human face betrays multiple thoughts and feelings. The card challenges my thinking.

• The face is being covered because of shame. I cannot face what I have done.

• The face is showing disbelief, or is this an expression of amazement?

• The hand can be seen as stroking the face in a gesture of affection or, in the alternative, slapping it in anger.

• Another way of looking at the card is to see the right hand as making the Sign of the Cross, a blessing of the self. I let my mind open to these possibilities and to others.

Picture Card 32

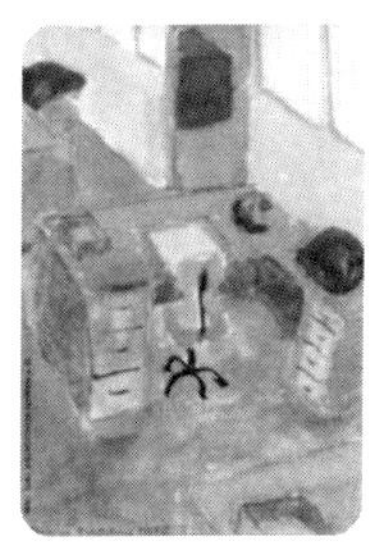

This is a work station. The in-basket is empty; the typewriter is covered. The secretary is absent. Either it is before or after the workday. In any event no work is being done and none is contemplated. A secretary's life is one of sameness, yesterday's work is the same as today's and tomorrow's. A secretary is responsible for transforming the spoken word into the written word. Another function of the secretary is to record permanently the decisions which have been made by the group.

• By drawing this card I understand that I am under a work imperative. There is much work to be done. The card is signaling a need for me to begin my work at once. In the Roman Catholic monastic orders, members are required to say a regular set of prayers each day. It is called the daily office. This card means performing a regularized function in life as part of my duty.

Picture Card 33

In *Proverbs 6:6*, one is exhorted to work as hard as the ant and to be wise. The Talmud says that the ant teaches honesty. The ant is the symbol of hard work. A colony of ants signifies the organization of a community into a cohesive whole. Every ant has a specified duty. Improvisation is not tolerated. This assures the survival and continuation of the species. In the world of ants, the life span of the males is short-lived, but it is long enough to perform its sole function of impregnating the Queen to perpetuate the colony.

• In juxtaposition to the ants in the card is a tree whose roots go deep into the bowels of the Earth just as do the ants. The roots of the tree do the same work as the ants. Both work to bring nourishment to the communal body. This card informs and instructs me that my role in life is specialized and well-suited for me. If I am an ant there is no need to become a root.

• In some societies barren women sit on an anthill to become fertile. Elsewhere dirt taken from an anthill is used in rituals used in connection with the stomach and for better digestion. The ants symbolize the inner workings of the bowels in the Earth. In Morocco there was a time when live ants were given to one suffering from sleeping sickness to swallow.

• Alternatively, the ants are at a picnic or perhaps they are preparing for the winter.

• When one is said to have ants in the pants, it means that the person has an excessive amount of eagerness. A Chinese proverb said that if you are patient in one moment of emotion, you will escape a hundred days of sorrow.

Picture Card 34

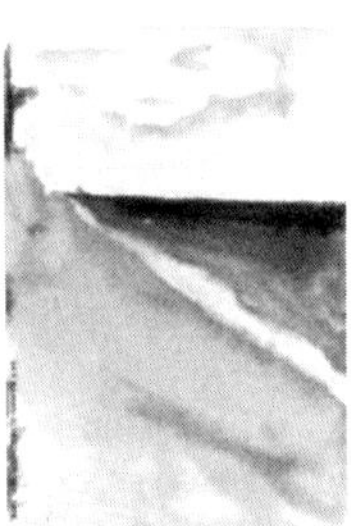

When I contemplate sand and the ocean, I have a sense of a world without end. Sand shifts like opinions. Dry, sand can be carried on the wind; wet, it can be formed and shaped. It has the attributes of both a fluid and a solid. Yet it is neither. The ocean speaks its mood, now gentle, now seething. All its individual drops appear to be a solid and in waves become a spray.

• When I lie upon the sand, it conforms to the shape of my body. It becomes a warm and safe place and is a womb symbol. It is my place to meditate upon the vastness of the universe of my being. Like the infinite number of grains of sand, I have an infinite number of ideas.

• Sand lies between land and water, between the conscious and the unconscious. Typically, a beach is devoid of vegetation, signifying an absence of life while life teems in the realms it borders.

• The sea is the symbol of the unconscious. It is vast and deep and lays claim to the land. Sharks and death rise from its depths as do life and pearls. The unconscious, like the sea, is the place where life is formed and surfaces to become the experience of the conscious world, the moving tides of life and my patterned existence.

• When Jonah was swallowed by the whale, he was more than simply a prisoner. According to Paracelsus, Jonah saw "mighty mysteries," during his three-day stay. A commentary by Rabbi Elieser compared Jonah's entry into the whale to a man entering a great synagogue. The whale's two eyes were like windows through which light shone illuminating Jonah. Jonah could look out through the whale's eyes and see everything in the depths of the ocean, suggesting a metaphor for the unconscious. By "mysteries," Paracelsus meant symbols which he saw as a means of expression. He felt that they were bridges which transport a person from the corporeal to the spiritual, much like the advice of Jesus to Nicodemus to be born again. (*John* 3:1).

• Alternatively, the beach is pleasant and warm. It is a peaceful day and this is a place of relaxation. When I need to cool down, I walk to the water´s edge and dive in for a swim or to float and enjoy the life of this moment. Don't make waves. Don't make sand.

Picture Card 35

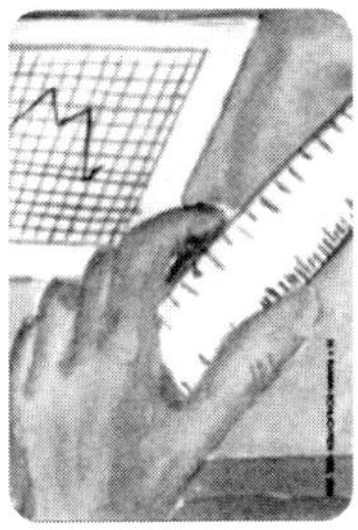

The ruler is symbolic of measuring up, asking whether I have completed the task I started. The graph represents my report card. Sometimes I measure up and finish what I started and at other times my efforts fail. This card asks me to take an objective measure of my self and others. This will allow me to assess my subjective ideas, preconceived notions, and prejudices. It is enough to determine whether I am just and whether I am harmonious within and without.

• The graph is a metaphor for the changes which are always occurring in my life. I am reminded that ups and downs are natural variations.

Picture Card 36

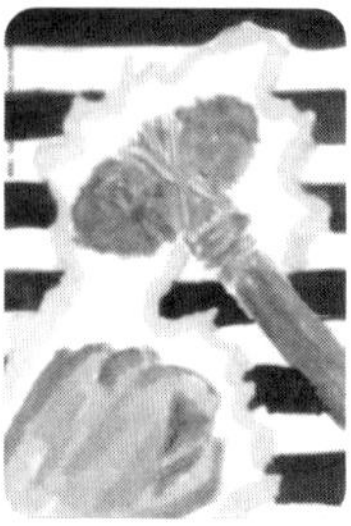

The stone axe symbolizes rolling thunder in thick clouds. The jagged yellow surrounding the stone axe and the clenched fist represent a thunderbolt. The stone axe connotes something evil and menacing. The head of the stone axe contains the blood of its victims. It has broken through the bars and is ready for another assault. The clenched left fist signals resolve and aggression. It is the symbol of a demand for liberation. A stone axe can be a creator or a destroyer. Its purpose here is clear. The thunderbolt has been forged. Blood has been spilled.

• According to Mayan mythology, the stone axe fell from heaven. It has the power to make it rain or to make the rain stop if it rains too much. The stone axe may be a symbol of wrath and destruction or it may be a symbol of resistance to malevolent forces.

• This card is an image of deep feelings of hostility and the urge to attack. To work through feelings, I sit alone either outdoors or in my study and place an empty chair in front of me. I image the person for whom I feel this enmity and I apologize! It does not matter that I was right and the other person was wrong. I hold my hands on my knees palms up and feel the hands of the other in mine. I image the flames rising from my heart and feel the energy coursing up through my shoulders, down my arms, exiting my palms, and passing swiftly into the other person. At this moment I realize the healing energy of love and the feelings of hostility dissolve.

• Alternatively, do I have an axe to grind? Is it time to turn to more productive thoughts and activities?

• Note: *Isaiah* 2:4 "... and they shall beat their swords into plowshares, and their spears into pruning hooks . . ." and the contrast in *Joel* 3:10: "Beat your plowshares into swords, and your pruning hooks into spears." The stone axe: Now a weapon, now a tool.

• This card pictures a medical utensil being used on a patient or as portrayal of the instrument by which a crime was perpetrated.

Picture Card 37

Hands are sometimes compared with the eye. Both see. The eye sees an action to perform and the hand does it as though it, too, sees. This notion is expressed as eye/hand coordination. Hands rather than eyes are more expressive of my true identity. The movement of my hands add tangible meaning to my verbal and nonverbal expressions.

My words of hello or goodbye are made firm with the gesture. The open palm with extended fingers signal warmth and peace. All civilizations use hands as language.

• Hands are instruments for transferring healing power of the indwelling reservoir of spirit.

• The hand of justice metes out the spirit of the law.

• The card is a reminder that all expression is self-directed. The person on the vehicle is not my mirror-image. Yet I am receiving the same expression as the one I am giving. When I curse another, I am cursing myself. When I bless another, I am blessing myself. Remembering and practicing this simple axiom, that all expression is self-directed, will change my life for the better.

• I have to ask myself whether this is a regularly scheduled bus which makes stops or a chartered bus running for me alone. If this is a school bus I am on the way to a place of learning. Perhaps it is a sightseeing bus. If I am on the ground, I must ask myself whether I am leaving the best part of myself behind.

Picture Card 38

Since all human brains are wired the same way, phenomena such as rainbows have a universality of symbolism. We give names to colors and symbolic meanings to colors in common. We engage in visual self-deception in common and deceive ourselves in common with all our sense organs. This is the basis for the common thread which runs through all symbols no matter the culture, the geography, or the age in which I find myself.

Over the ages and through the many cultures and countries, the rainbow has come to symbolize things to come, both good and bad. It is closely related to the cycle of rebirth, *metempsychosis*.

In the Chinese language there are five ideograms which denote rainbows. All five contain the root *ho-i*, which means serpent. African Pygmies call the rainbow the perilous sky-serpent. They see a solar arch formed by a pair of serpents. Another culture sees the rainbow as a mighty python who slithers into the sky to take a bath. The python gleams brightly and frolics in the bath. He tips water from the bath and it becomes sun-rain, hazardous water for human beings. The Incas would not gaze upon a rainbow. When one appeared they covered their mouths with their hands. In Central Asia there is a general belief that rainbows suck up the rivers and lakes and drink the water. Another group feels that rainbows suck up children into the heavens.

• Yet the other meaning of the rainbow, that it predicts good things, persists mainly because the rainbow is seen as a bridge. It is a crossing to the Good. Just as it can symbolize approaching disturbances, it also symbolizes approaching happiness. The serpent is constantly changing. Rainbows came to symbolize serpents because they too indicate change. In China, the rainbow and Eros are closely tied together because it is the rainbow which is the link between Heaven and Earth. Heaven and Earth are the principles of yin and yang and the rainbow therefore is the symbol of the feeling connection or the Eros dimension. The spectrum of the rainbow has a numbered order, a specified number of colors always in the same order. The rainbow represents in this sense a set of feeling-time-numbers.

• When I draw this card I am acknowledging the duality of life on Earth. In *Genesis* 9:12-13, God offers the rainbow as a token of the covenant between God and the Earth to maintain equanimity of existence. Whatever is happening now, the card says, the bridge can be crossed, the river can be forded, and the rainbow is my sign that this is true.

• Water gathers in two main states, either as stagnant waters or as moving waters. Stagnant waters are generally self-contained and come in greatly varying sizes. Ponds are stagnant as are lakes. Rivers, streams, and oceans are examples of moving waters. They flow. They ebb. Pictured in this card is a river. The river is always moving. It is confined by its banks which give the river its sense of direction. The river always follows the exact same pathway.

• The river symbolizes a parade, a demonstration or a procession. It is a movement such as the Civil Rights Movement. It moves inexorably to its goal. It is the stage prior to the riot which is typified by the river going into a flood stage. Here though the river is controlling itself, moving easily between its banks, witnessed only by the silent trees on the shores.

Picture Card 39

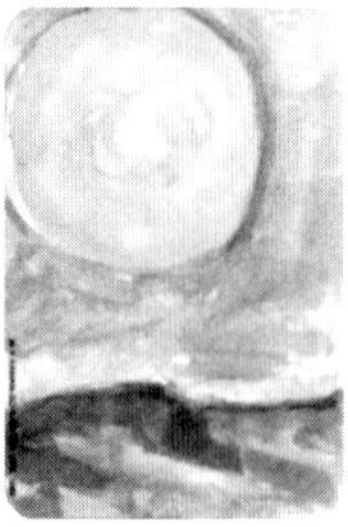

Tribes which have survived from ancient times, like Aborigines, Pygmies and Bushmen, look upon the Sun as the Eye of God. It is God's good eye. The Moon is God's evil eye. Our Sun provides light, heat, and life. On the other hand the Sun can bring about drought, even floods. Yet there are billions of suns in the heavens, stars constantly being born, burning brightly for eons, and then dying. Our Sun is no different. One day it will die as well and our light, heat, and life will disappear. The Moon has no light of its own. It merely reflects the light of the Sun. Its symbol reflects dependence, the female principle, and periodic change. These are the symbols of the rhythms of life, from birth to death.

• Applying numerology, the Sun is One and the Moon is Two. It is notable that light always follows darkness in the order of cosmic development. Light and darkness are the first cosmic duality. It is yin and yang. Just as yin always contains traces of yang and yang always has traces of yin, so too do light and darkness always have traces of each other. Because the Sun has such a dramatic impact on our lives, many solar rituals sprang up in early civilizations. Daily human sacrifices were made to the Sun. The blood of the victims was needed to feed the Sun. Sun worship produced civilizations of fear.

• Given this history of its symbolism, what does the Sun signify to me in this card? First, it signifies the Power of Light, the revelation I receive when I commune with my own dark side. When my unconscious unfolds and I acknowledge and embrace the buried part of my psyche, I am re-created. All secret societies have initiation rites which symbolize light coming into the life of the initiated and creating a new person. Second, the card signifies the bringing of order out of chaos, things in my life straightening themselves out; decadence becoming spirituality; disintegration becoming unity. Finally, the card symbolizes the creative spark which I carry with me always. All Egyptian mummies had an amulet symbolizing the Sun. This spark is with you no matter where you are or what your condition might be. In *John* 1:9, Jesus says, "I am the Light of the World." I am the Light of my world. I have no limitation except that which I impose upon myself.

Picture Card 40

The absolute and final conclusion of anything or anybody is called death. Death never takes a holiday. It is pervasive in so many ways that hardly a day passes without my observance of it. The animal and plants I ate for dinner were once alive. Now they are dead. Friendships and relationships I once had are now over.

• All secret societies incorporate the death ritual in the initiation – *mors junua vitae* — death is the Gate of Life. Death opens the doors to the spirit world. When I am initiated I undergo great change. It is profound. Death is called the Daughter of Night and the Sister of Sleep. When I am asleep I mimic the death state.

• I agonize over death. I view it with fear. Yet it is not death I fear. My fear really is more of a resistance to change from the known to the unknown. Death absorbs me into nothingness. Nothing can possibly happen to me after death. I relax. However, when I encounter a dead end in my daily life, it means that changes are about to occur. The suggestion of this card is that I should stop my resistance to change.

• There are no extremes as opposite as Life and Death; not even the gulf between rich and poor or full and empty can approach the chasm that separates that which is alive from that which is dead. The thread between life and death is fragile. How can two states be so distant and yet so connected that the thinnest of threads divides them? The answer is that each partakes of the other. It is this way with all extremes, the farther apart they appear to me the more they participate in the attributes of their opposite.

• Alternatively, someone once said that all death is suicide. A self-abusive lifestyle such as one with heavy use of alcohol or drugs is such a lifestyle. There is also a spiritual death (*Romans* 8:6) about which Paul warned.

Picture Card 41

Like the bum, the prostitute is a person of great power. She bears the energy of a goddess. No matter that she is diseased or an addict. No matter that she has no feelings for me or emotional tie to me. She allows me to share her energy. There is no such thing as perversion with her. I am free to release my most secret fantasy without any fear. The card symbolizes union with my dark side which will bring about wholeness of my being.

• Judah had three sons, Er, Onan, and Shelah. Er married Tamar. Er died prematurely, before Tamar had conceived a child. Under the law of the times, Onan was required to impregnate Tamar so that Er could have an heir. Onan though did not think much of the idea and spilled his seed. (The term "onanism" is derived from his name.) He, too, died prematurely. Fearful that the third son would suffer the same fate, Judah sent Tamar to live with her father, promising that when Shelah was old enough he would perform the levirate duty and marry her.

Later when Judah was traveling in the countryside he met Tamar who had disguised herself as a prostitute. Judah slept with her and did not recognize her since her face was covered. Judah promised to send her a baby goat from his flock. To guarantee it, he left her his signet and his cord.

When he sent the kid, the whore could not be found. Later when Tamar's pregnancy became common knowledge, Judah condemned her and ordered her brought before him for sentencing. When Judah asked his daughter-in-law to identify her lover she said that she was pregnant "By the man whose these are, am I with child," and she showed Judah his signet and the cord.

Judah, of course, admitted that Tamar was more moral than he. (*Genesis*: 38)

• This card invites the same comparison of moralities. In the picture, is it the whore or the trick who is more moral? Or, in a parallel situation, how do I judge? Should I judge?

• This card refers to a removal of strictures such as a refusal to abide by commands of parents, dictates of law enforcement, obedience to the morality of the culture, or even civil disobedience. In the card the prostitute no longer equates sex with morals – sexuality and morality are unrelated according to this philosophy of life. The same would hold true when this principle is applied in other phases of life. For instance, the strictures could be in place because of a sense of loyalty to one's elders such as a rule prohibiting associating with certain groups.

• Prostitution becomes more commonplace when there is a population imbalance such as during a war or when fewer marriageable men are in the pool. When it overwhelms a community, either police action is stepped up or prostitution is limited to certain geographic areas.

Picture Card 42

When I draw this card, I ask myself what am I seeking at the altar where I worship?

This card looks to me like a place of worship and sacrifice, the interior of a church or temple. At the top of the card is a "stained glass window" of four equilateral triangles which suggest to me a dodecahedron. The dodecahedron is a solid face which has 12 plane faces, a polygon in shape. The dodecahedron derives its meaning and symbolism from Pythagoras. Plato in the Timaeus believed it to be the shape of the cosmos.

• The altar which I see in this card is the temple in microcosm. The altar is the entire temple. Sacrifice is the ritual which makes things holy and the altar is the sacred place where sacrifice takes place just as the temple was when it existed. The altar is raised above everyone and everything. The purpose of the altar is spiritualization of the world. On the altar in the card is a tabernacle, the most sacred and the most holy place. The Ancient Egyptians kept the statues of their Gods in such a holy place. The Temple in Jerusalem contained the Ark of the Covenant and the *Urim* and *Thummim*, the oracle which spoke the words of God. The object of the Tabernacle is to trap the power which comes from God and hold it within a space intended for human beings.

The temptation is to use the knowledge I have of the power of the dodecahedron for magic or for acquiring material things. The symbol is meant to lead me to a mystical view of Nature. It is a perversion to make it into an idol and to use it for purposes of worship. The candles symbolize divine light. The wick and the wax symbolize flesh and the flame symbolizes spirit. Both the wick and the wax are consumed by the flame.

• As with all the cards, what I see will not always correspond to what you see. When I first encountered this card I saw it as a birthday cake, the symbol of the fulfillment of my wishes. The interpretation of the card though remained the same: What am I seeking? Images flip; meanings do not.

• Other random images may flow from the various uses of an altar. An altar is a raised structure upon which a sacrifice takes place. Am I to be sacrificed? One burns incense at an altar to worship a Deity. Is my faith being challenged?

• In Christian churches it is called variously the Lord's Table or the Communion Table. Past memories will trigger new images. Secret societies use altars in their rituals. Thoughts of promises and loyalty are reawakened.

• Another slant on this card is the story of Hannukah. Over 2000 years ago the Syrian King Antrochus IV occupied Jerusalem. The Jews were required to worship Greek Gods. Judah the Maccabee was the leader of a rebellion against the Syrians. He led the Jews to victory over the Syrians. When they reclaimed the Temple it had to be rededicated. First they cleaned it thoroughly from top to bottom and then they lit the Menorah, a candelabrum. Enough oil for only one day was found. It would take eight days to fetch new oil. Inexplicably, the small amount of oil lasted eight days. The significance of the card is the idea of rededication, getting back to old vows, renewing past promises, acclaiming old holidays and celebrations.

• This card may signify a call to the altar, emphasizing that the vocation to become a religious is very real indeed.

• I close my eyes and look deep inside the circle. Within this circle are drawn four triangles. It has a golden center, indicating its value. Underneath the golden center are written Hebrew letters and Latin words. The seal bears a relationship to hidden powers. It can be used to inspire love or to cast spells.

Picture Card 43

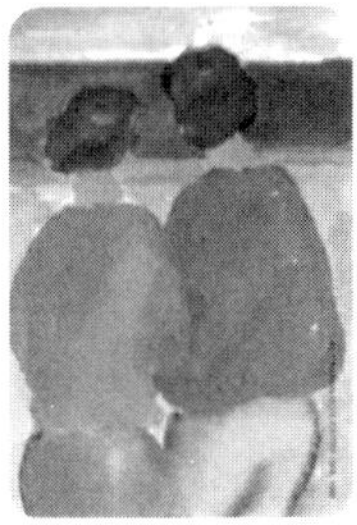

This card symbolizes the deeper significance and definition of male and female. My soul, my indwelling spirit, is a combination of male and female elements. To confine my understanding of the distinctions to biological differences would be to miss the broader context.

• In many early creation myths, the first human being is an hermaphrodite. When the separation takes place, the distinction between male and female begins. Mystics regard the spirit as male and the soul as female. These are expressed as the *animus/anima* duality. These terms do not denote sexuality. The fact that I live in a world which defines itself in sexual terms is confusing. It is a block to a comprehension of the giving/receiving process.

• The animus has a shadow, the dark masculine. When I am terrorized in a dream by a male monster or when a male creature in a horror movie frightens me, I am experiencing a tickling of the dark side of my animus. The same applies to the anima and its dark side, the dark feminine.

• The Greek name for the Earth was *chthonos*, mother of the Titans. It was the place which combines the living and the dead. It stands for the dark side of the Earth. The adjective, chthonian, developed to mean dragons and serpents, monsters which were born in the underworld. Things chthonian came to signify the threatening side of the battle between the forces of life and death. The unconscious has a chthonian aspect which produces unforeseen disaster, a lack of confidence and fear. Anything which frightens me by its suddenness, its violence, and its overwhelming strength is chthonian.

The chthonian female is the shadow of the anima and the chthonian male is the shadow of the animus. When either of these aspects become constellated I can go in one of two directions: Either I can move into the final phase of my personal development and achieve a soul-nourishing relationship with the Transcendent, or I can move into the dregs and drudgery of a difficult existence.

• This card reminds me that there is more to me than I, female, or I male, that my sexual leanings are no more important than my food appetites. The experiences which promote wholeness are meditation and regular use of the oracle. Through these vehicles I will have visions and revelations; I will enhance my relationship with others; I will know my destiny and understand my patterning.

• Does the word female derive from the word male? Does the word woman derive from man? Or is the reverse the truth? Does man come from woman and male from female?

• Unlike the river which is always moving in a particular direction, the ocean derives its direction from the winds which blow upon it. Also unlike the river, the ocean has a voice and a mood. Its mood is determined by its voice. It can be angry or it can be regular and pleasant. It is always persistent. For 24 hours each day, the sound never stops. It never dissipates. It exists forever. It touches the land where I am and the land where there are foreigners.

• In Greek mythology, the story is told of Ianthe, a beautiful young girl from Crete who fell in love with a girl named Iphis. The mother of Iphis, Telethusa, had been ordered by the father to kill the child if it was a girl. Her motherly instinct won out over her sense of obedience to her husband and she pretended that her child was a boy. Telethusa maintained her daughter's secret and raised her as a boy, even giving her a boy's name (Iphis). Seeing what she perceived as an unconditional love between Ianthe and Iphis, Telethusa implored the goddess Aphrodite to change Iphis into a male. She did so and the lovers were soon thereafter married.

All such same sex relationships do not end so triumphantly. Until recently, disclosure of the existence of such a union was bound to cause reprisals. The comparative ease with which gays and lesbians move in some circles today masks the irrational fear harbored by some. The fear arises from the attacker's imagined involvement in the lifestyle viewed as aberrant.

• When an older gay male is the mentor or leader of a group of younger homosexuals, he is called the mother.

•When used in a derogatory way, the word mother means a despicable person.

Picture Card 44

There was a time in the twentieth century, believe it or not, when there was no white line down the center of the highway. It was not until around 1914 that the white line was conceptualized. Until highways got their white lines, chaos ruled. The white line down the center of a highway represents the concept of the rule. I use a rule (or ruler) to draw a straight line. Because the ruler produces a straight line, it has come to signify righteousness. Without the ruler, plans for building construction could not have been drawn. Structures such as the Egyptian pyramids could not have been built. The white line in the card signifies making perfect. Without the ruler, laborers would work at random. Without the white line, cars would drive at random. There would be no cohesion.

Every religious order has what is called its rule, the written vehicle for its governance, like a constitution. The rule of an order is written by founders, such as St. Benedict, St. Theresa of Avila, St. Dominic, and St. Augustine. St.

Augustine said that all things have been made to a rule. A good example of the extension of the concept of the rule into everyone's life is the United States Constitution which is the rule for Americans. Every organization has by-laws. So too must I have a rule. My plans for building my life, to make my life perfect, are my rule. It is up to me to paint a white line down my own road of life.

Picture Card 45

A game becomes a universe unto itself. When I find myself in a game, I have to find the role I am supposed to play, like it or not. All games have images and symbols. All games have a predetermined setting. Baseball has a diamond and football has its 100 yards as examples. Most games have rules and a wholeness. What I see in games are models of life. A game is the reverse of anarchy. It is the model of an organized civilization. Cunning and individual spontaneity can enable me to defeat a more skilled opponent.

Even when I am the only one playing the game as are the two children in the card, the game has the same components as an organized team game. When I am flying a kite I am magically wandering through the clouds. The child playing with a doll is unconsciously reenacting fertility rites. In this card, the child on the swing feels the exhilaration of going up as a result of the effort put out when down. The child on the slide is copying the behavior of adults. Going to work is the equivalent of climbing the ladder and then reaping the benefit by gliding down successfully.

The game I play will charge me emotionally and activate my imagination. The games children play are the same games adults play. All human relations have a game component within them.

Games develop my spontaneity, making me more instinctive. They prepare me for all of life's activities. When I draw this card I always give vent to my urge to play for self-development. I pick the game which reflects me and my patterning: Monopoly®, Trivial Pursuit®, snorkeling, sky diving, computer games or Rubik's Cube®. Any of them will do since the way I play awakens me to my real identity.

- In the game of life, what role am I playing?
- By whose rules am I playing?

Picture Card 46

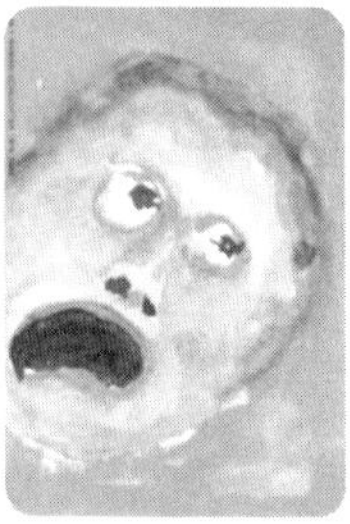

Into the mouth go air and food. These become the breath and the nourishment so necessary for life. From the mouth come words. Just as the air I breathe and the food I consume can be life-enhancing or putrid and stale, so too can the words which flow from my mouth be elevating and animating or destructive and debasing.

For Greek philosophers, *logos*, which means word, stands for more than just the words I speak. It also means reason, intellect, and divine thought. These give logos power. The power derives not from the speaker who is intrinsically powerless, but rather from the words themselves which in and of themselves are an act or an event, a happening. Thus the blessing or the curse derives its power from the Deity or the Totem which is invoked.

Words are the continuous creation or destruction of the universe. What I say is a manifestation of me. Every expression is self-directed. The card presents the image of the mouth of darkness. This is a chthonian symbol, the entrance to the netherworld. It symbolizes the movement from day to night, life to death, light to darkness. The eyes are the symbols of the receipt of light and represent intellectual perception. In the cards the eyes are expressing what the mouth is saying.

• Each century gains a reputation. The twentieth century was remarkable not only for its great progress in saving lives and making life more bearable but also because of the violent killings of masses which took place. In the Ukraine, Kulaks were hunted down and killed. Armenians fell at the hands of the Turks. Hitler's Germany massacred Jews and others. In Bosnia many Muslims were murdered as were Tutsis in Rawanda.

• This card reminds me that not only centuries but also moments, days, months, and years have reputations. How I live moment to moment determines my legacy.

• When I am torn between sensual cravings and the necessity of living in a practical manner, I am likely to become restless. A lack of patience will be a major obstacle in building a good marriage or a permanent relationship.

Picture Card 47

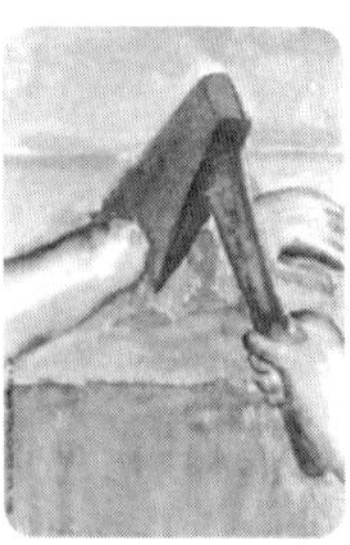

The need is to recognize the dichotomy between the conscious, as represented by the right hand, and the unconscious, as represented by the left hand. My conscious mind is taking over and dominating my life. I need to meditate and engage in rituals in order to restore a balance between the conscious and the unconscious. Working with my dreams is also a good method for achieving inner harmony. This image is a metaphor for the power of differentiation.

• *Matthew* 18:9 states, "And if thine eye offend thee, pluck it out, and cast it from thee." In some cultures, the punishment for theft is dismemberment. The card indicates an activity marked by suddenness, from which there will be severe consequences and sorrow.

Picture Card 48

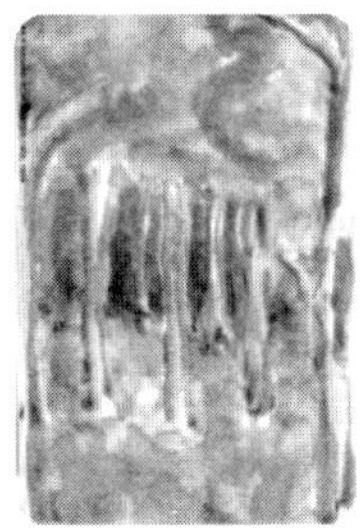

The tree is a symbol of life and the cyclical nature of the tree symbolizes the life and death cycle. It participates in three worlds: It lives upon the Earth's surface, recording all important events on its annual rings. Second, it reaches into the heavens seizing the light and spreading it through its branches and leaves. Third, its roots burrow deep into the ground. When it dies it sinks deep into the Earth and thousands of years later it becomes coal.

• Serpents crawl among its roots; animals scamper up its trunk and birds nest in its branches. The tree brings all this together. Its bloodstream is the water it sucks up from the ground and turns into sap. Its body is the trunk; its branches are its arms. It breathes and bends with the wind. No wonder then that the tree became one of the world's earliest oracles.

• The German Black Forest has the mystical quality of the unknown. It is deep and impenetrable. The woods in fairy tales represent the home of mysterious and sometimes frightening characters. But mostly, masses of trees bring peace. Animals who live in lowlands where there are no trees are bellicose. Animals who dwell in forests are more placid. This applies to human beings as well. To draw this card is an invitation to enter the placid world of trees, to cool my temper and my anxiety and to figuratively hug a tree. When I rub two pieces of tree together I can produce fire. Thus each of the four elements are present in a tree: fire, water, air, and earth. In addition to having all four elements at work, the tree is also the world's calendar. Through its annual rings it records catastrophes and cataclysms. It records bountiful times and lean times, the good and the bad. The tree is a book of harmony and peace, a witness of my times.

• Each tree in a forest keeps a diary of the major events which have occurred during its lifetime. The annual rings within a tree's trunk are the calendar by which cataclysms are noted. Does such a calendar exist within me?

• It is difficult to travel through a forest because of its depth and its density.

The trees overhang and form a kind of rooftop, making the forest a dwelling into which you have wandered.

• When I am alone in a forest, the trees become the pillars and columns of a sacred place. I am in a sanctuary.

• The forest is inhabited by a spirit. Two Tlingit Native American clans in Alaska honor this tradition. When one clan needs a new building they ask the other clan to do the construction. They then weave blankets and collect dried fish for the workers. When the building is completed, both clans thank the spirit of the forest for the lumber. At the dedication of the building, the builders sit in the center of the new building as guests of honor.

• It is also possible to see the forest as a giant army with each tree as a stalwart soldier.

Picture Card 49

The male in the picture is far larger, disproportionately so, than the female. These represent the male and female energies within me. The myth I am most familiar with which deals with these energies is the Adam and Eve story. The male energy as represented by Adam is the rational force. The female energy is the creative force. All sin arises in the female side, since rationality does not admit of activities off the beaten path. The Hebrew word for sin means to miss the mark. The masculine energy never misses the mark. The feminine energy acts without the mark in mind. Thus, in the Adam and Eve myth, it is the feminine which approaches the masculine with the idea of eating the apple. The non sense arises in the female element. The sense arises in the male. Carl Jung said that the pendulum of the mind oscillates more between sense and non sense than it does between good and bad. The couple pictured in the card represent this dichotomy.

•Jealousy is an ancient sensation. Originally it pertained to feelings held by a man about a woman to whom he was married. Torah described the method utilized by Hebrews under Mosaic law. *Numbers* 5:11-31 lays out the ritual which the priest followed whenever a husband felt his wife had strayed. A bitter potion was mixed and the wife was required to drink it. According to the legend, her belly would swell and her thigh would rot if she had been unfaithful.

• The couple in the card portray a man who appears to be menacing a smaller female. Jealousy is a prime cause for disruptive behavior in the male/

female relationship. The ancient ritual was not much more effective in settling problems of jealousy than are today's. Whether jealousy is my problem or if my partner is jealous of me, jealousy appears to be an ancient notion which has emerged from the unconscious.

• Jealousy is an infantile reaction. When it arises, I ask myself about childhood fantasies I once had about wanting to get rid of someone (even a parent) in order to have exclusive relations with another. These childhood feelings have surfaced again, except that the cast of characters has changed.

Picture Card 50

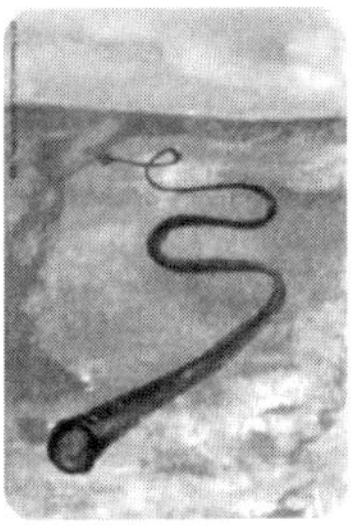

Besides being the symbol for authority, the whip also symbolizes the things I must do to drive out the demons which haunt me. My fears, my suspicions, and my blockages to learning appear as the demons of my dreams and my imaginings. The whip is the symbol of the corrections I want to bring about in my life. I want to exercise my second sight. I want to meditate and pray with regularity. I want to open up to myself. I lift up the whip and use it on myself.

• Daedalus was the architectural engineer who created the first labyrinth. King Minos imprisoned certain Athenians in the labyrinth, feeling that it was escape proof. When King Minos heard that the Athenians had gotten out, he was convinced that only Daedalus could have engineered their escape. Accordingly King Minos imprisoned Daedalus and his son Icarus in the labyrinth, proof of its excellent design since even the maker of the labyrinth could not find the exit without outside help.

In order to escape, Daedalus, ever the inventor, made a pair of wings for himself and a pair for his son. He told Icarus to follow him in a middle course flying over the sea, warning Icarus that if he flew too close to the Sun, the glue would melt and the wings would drop off. Once in the air, Icarus disregarded his father's orders and flew so close to the Sun that the glue melted and the wings came off. Icarus fell into the sea and drowned. The body of water into which he fell is named for him. It is called the Icarian Sea.

• The discipline imposed by parental authority is designed to save a child from potential disaster. Thus the expression: Spare the rod; spoil the child. The whip represents discipline in its most extreme form. I do not need such a device to enforce discipline upon myself or upon others. Discipline arises out of respect for authority.

• Seen as a tube, the object is a symbol of that which is transported to the place where it is needed.

• When I see the object as a rope, it could mean a release or rescue, I am no longer tied up.

• Seen as a microphone, the card is signaling an announcement.

Picture Card 51

The serpent is cold-blooded; it has no arms or legs, no hair or feathers. Yet in the chain of evolution the serpent is one of my earliest progenitors. I am at the opposite end of the chain of evolution from the serpent. There is something of the serpent in everyone. Centuries before Darwin's studies, ancients recognized intuitively that there were some connections between human beings and the serpent. The Chaldeans, as an example, had one word for serpent and life. In Arabic the word for serpent is *el-hayyah* while the word for life is *el-hayat*. One of God's principal names is *El-Hay* which means life-giving in the sense of one who is the principle of life.

• The part of the serpent which resonates in the human being is the libido, that part of me over which I have no control. It represents my lower psyche. The symbol of the serpent is of one who is holy and yet not spiritual. The serpent is so swift that it eludes time which can be clocked, space which can be measured, and logic which can be reasoned. The serpent symbolizes that which changes from female to male and back again, that which is secret, here one moment gone the next, through my fingers and gone. The serpent represents the continuous transformation of death into life and life into death. It is an ongoing revolution. The serpent sheds its outer skin every year and becomes a new individual. The card signals major changes in my life.

• The serpent is limbless, but no one sees the serpent as helpless. Its hissing, its ability to bite, and venom are enough to frighten its prey or its predators. Without limbs, the serpent can climb higher than the monkey; it can outswim a fish and it can outleap a kangaroo. Its strength and its guile have given the snake a bad reputation. At the same time, the symbol of a serpent with its tail in its mouth is a symbol of eternity, symbolizing how the serpent came to represent wisdom in the East.

• All of this illustrates how an image is able to convey such divergent symbols. For this reason it is important to expand your view of each symbol. My first impression of this card is that of a snake in the grass. For some people that is as far as they need to go. If I get an emotional reaction when I see "a snake in the grass," if my stomach knots up, I am in the right arena. I am dealing with my characteristic of going after others from a position of stealth. On the other hand if I get no emotional reaction from the "snake in the grass" reading, I have to look at other potential meanings.

• The serpent represents the astrological sign of Scorpio. Sometimes a fireworks display twists as it burns, much like a serpent. A piece of jewelry done in the shape of a serpent might bring to mind an emotional encounter once had with its wearer. The image might bring to mind the antidote needed after a bite by a venomous serpent.

• Each spring, the serpent sheds its skin and is completely renewed. Each of us can do the same thing, undergo periodic renewal.

• Finally the serpent has the ability to hypnotize its prey.

• When I use the serpent as a symbol I go inside the serpent's skin; I learn to hypnotize others and I understand what it means to be a limbless serpent.

• Legend has it that originally the serpent had the power of speech and of all the animals was the most intelligent. The serpent saw itself in competition with the human beings. In the Biblical story of Eve and the serpent (*Genesis* 3) the serpent projects his envy of man by suggesting in verse 5 that God does not want to share fruit from the tree of knowledge of good and evil because once man eats it he will be the same as God.

• When I read this card I consider such a projection as a possibility, especially if the scenario involves competitive forces.

Picture Card 52

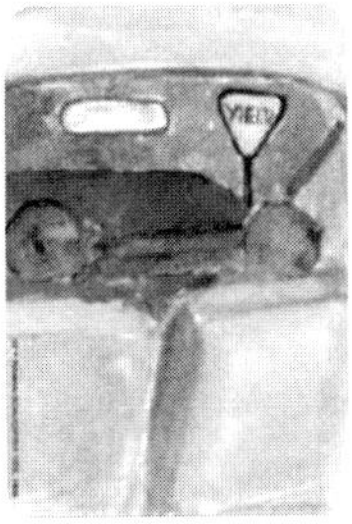

The worldwide system of traffic signs is a good example of the creation of a modern ideographic system. In the world of ideographic traffic symbols the shape of the sign is the ideogram which sends the message. I know what the sign is saying the moment I see its shape. With its point going downward the triangle has a negative spectrum of meanings. Alchemically it represents water which is the passive element. Hobo signs exist as an ideographic system also. Hoboes leave signs on doorposts, walls, and other surfaces. These signs give information about the place and the people where the sign is placed. The upside down triangle is a hobo sign. It means *no good, too many have been here.* As a traffic sign, the reversed triangle means *be passive, yield, or give way to crossing traffic.* By drawing this card I am being advised to let the game of life come to me rather than rushing in and trying to alter things. My patterning is fixed and by now I know where to put my passion. Now it is time to learn where I should post the sign of passivity.

Picture Card 53

The solitary tree stands in the meadow on a rise facing five red flowers. Trees have been accepted as oracles well before recorded history. Trees evolved on the earth 350 million years ago. When human beings began populating the Earth, they soon came to view trees as the homes of spirits able to communicate with them. Many people of antiquity accepted the tree as the symbol of the Macrocosm. While the tree is seen as active, flowers are viewed as passive. Flowers became symbols of the soul's virtues, of love and harmony. Made into a bouquet, they symbolize spiritual perfection. The tree on the other hand can never be arranged. It is majestic because of its size, its longevity, and its psychic qualities.

• The tree is a calendar, marking years with rings which tell of good times or cataclysmic years. The tree connects the underworld through its roots, with the Earth's surface through its trunk, and finally with the heavens through its branches. Snakes live in its roots, birds in its branches. Water circulates through the tree; the Earth feeds it; it breathes the air and it makes a fire. As much as the tree participates in wholeness, how much more so do I? The tree reminds me of who I am. The flowers adorn me. With this card I am asked to delve into my identity.

• A garden is always man-made because it is ordered and managed. Near a garden there are always people nearby who tend the garden.

• It is within the flower which is colorful that the reproductive cycle begins. The flower reminds me that my smile and friendly attitude will be repeated over and over by those who are inseminated by my flower-like approach.

• The tree has been thought to be solitary, with no brother or sister trees for companionship. Experimental studies have shown the opposite, that trees are in contact with other trees.

Picture Card 54

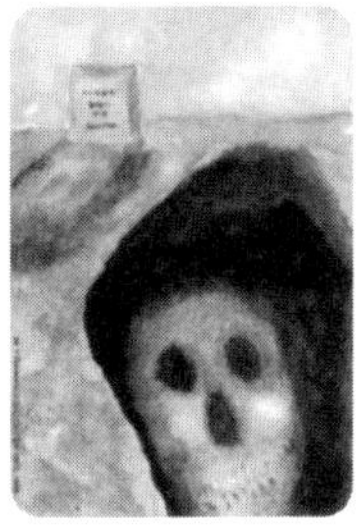

The bony frame of my face is called a skull. Ghosts are portrayed frequently with a skull in place of a face. The skull and crossbones is the pirates' symbol. It also stands for poison and for death itself.

The skull has come to signify death because one recognizes it as the most important part of a once-living person. The face is the first thing anyone sees of me. Ninety percent of what the other person who observes me sees is my face. When I see the skull I see my own face. The tremors I feel when I envision death occur because I am reminded of my own death.

• This could be regarded as symbolizing the agony and the terror of being absorbed into nothingness. Also it is the symbol of the inevitable evolution of everything material including relationships. The best example is the rite of initiation of all secret societies which includes a death-imitation ceremony. This symbolizes a new life. The card corresponds to the thirteenth major arcanum of the Tarot which bears no name since it carries the number thirteen. Death brings about the ambivalence of a heaven or a hell and therefore symbolizes entry into one of two quite different states.

• This card is a symbol of the elimination of that which creates disorder. The skeleton is smiling ironically as if it knows something special and important which I do not know. After death it has found out something which is a big secret. Can I fathom it?

• Duality is a function of everyday life. To experience life is to experience its dualities. That which is born will die. That which blesses also curses and that which curses also blesses.

Picture Card 55

Gift-giving at Christmas, Hanukkah, birthdays, graduation, or celebrating a new book release, or even for a new venture, descends from a very ancient ritual. At the time of a fresh cycle, ancients gave their first fruits to a god or a king. What they got in return was a sense of protection and a promise of abundance in the future. According to the legend, Cain and Abel brought their first fruits for sacrifice to the Deity. Abel gave all of his first fruits; Cain secretly withheld a part of his. God rejected Cain's sacrifice because it was not complete. Cain killed Abel ostensibly because Abel's sacrifice was accepted and his was not. Cain then became an *outcast.* The story of the first outcast is also the story of the first murder. (*Genesis* 4:1-16). Cain embodied both.

• When my patterning casts me as the outcast, it is a difficult role to play. His brother Abel is an aspect of Cain himself. Abel is the half of Cain which is willing to give God everything. Being an outcast means that I am not willing to give all of myself. Like Cain, I become self-protective and I withhold the best part of myself.

• Being the outcast means total separation even from self. What I withhold from others I withhold from my self. There is a great deal of suffering because I can never be a part of the whole when I am the outsider. I cannot ever reach my own inner being nor can I make myself whole. Conversation stops when I approach. I am not privy to inside information. Yet I must play the hand I was dealt. I am a leper when I find myself in the role of outsider. The key to normalcy is to discover the richness of the outcast role and to harmonize this part of me with the whole. How did I come to be ostracized? The key to understanding this process is in understanding myself. Primitive tribes cast out malevolent members. Modern groups who exile or excommunicate a member do so because of something the person has done or because of some condition the member has. An outcast cannot reenter the group. An outcast needs an inner friend more than anything. The greatest resources I have, outcast or not, do not come from the outside. They come from an inner process which is reflected in the outer. The card answers my cry of vulnerability by instructing me to find my inner helper.

• Cain and Abel made their offerings and Cain's was rejected because he wrongly withheld a portion. In a jealous rage, Cain killed Abel and became the first outcast.

Picture Card 56

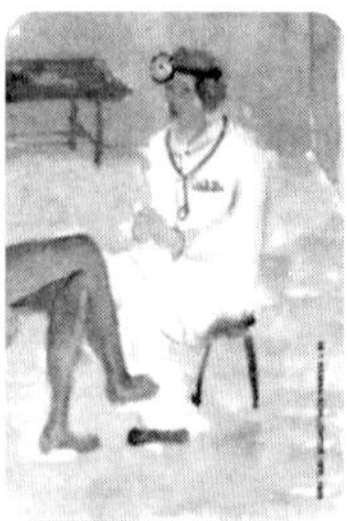

The stethoscope reminds me of a toy trumpet. The doctor uses it to examine my chest to listen to the sounds of my heart, my lungs, or other internal organs. The doctor has a standard by which my sounds are measured. If the sounds of my heart are muffled or if there is a gurgling in the lungs, the doctor is alerted.

• I carry an imaginary stethoscope with me whenever I encounter others. By their sounds I am able to decipher attitudes and predict behaviors. If I hear gruff words or detect scowls, I know I am dealing with cynicism. When I see tears and groans, I detect sadness and suffering. Evaluation of situations and of others is an ongoing human process. My task is to avoid making inaccurate judgments. The task is unlike the doctor's who must make a diagnosis, which is to make a judgment. My training leads me to be tolerant of differences. Judging ties me down to a single opinion and limits my growth. Everything contains its opposite. The worst cynic is also the greatest optimist. Therefore I use my stethoscope wisely, without making judgments about what I hear or see.

• The symbol which stands out in this card is the examination mirror on the doctor's forehead. This mirror is unlike any other. Its purpose is to reflect light on the subject for examination. There is a hole in the mirror through which the doctor peers. He or she aims the opening in the mirror at the patient's iris. The light the doctor needs to see fine details is reflected into the patient's eye by the mirror. It gathers the light and puts it on the subject. The symbolism is that the truth of what the heart holds is exposed. I reflect what is in my heart.

The stethoscope around the doctor's neck is used to listen to the rhythm of the heart. Since the heart is the center of the human body, it has become the symbol of feelings and intuition. When I set my heart upon a desire or when I meditate, I am speaking to my heart. The symbolism is asking whether my heart is responding as it should. Do I love with all of my heart? The promise is that if I need it, "A new heart also will I give you, and a new spirit I will put within you." (*Ezekiel* 36:26)

• A doctor is one who is skilled in the healing arts. Yet the doctor is a practitioner, one who is still seeking to expand knowledge and skill.

Picture Card 57

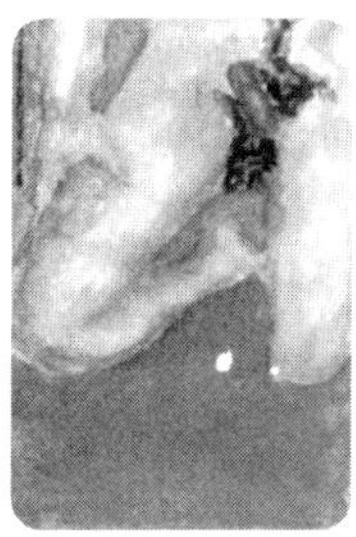

This card symbolizes the libido, my fundamental and basic energizing force. This is the force which drives the individual to action. What it is saying to me is that my potential can be realized at this moment. I am motivated to express myself. I can overcome any conflict or confrontation now. Libido is present in both males and females. If I speak in biological terms I become confused, not realizing that I am as much male as female.

To be a fully integrated individual I transcend my sexual identity. I do not remain fixed within it. Each of us goes through a phase of eroticism. Few of us escape it and move to the higher level where the libido serves us instead of being served by us. One is given the opportunity to disengage from the distinction between male and female. On this plane one begins to see things and grasp their symbolic meanings rather than living with their outer appearances.

• The story of Noah is the story of the first farmer. Noah is also credited with being the maker of the first calendar. (*Genesis* 9) He planted his first vineyard (*Genesis* 9: 20), harvested the grapes, and transformed the grapes into wine. He drank the wine, became drunk, fell asleep, and his erect penis was exposed. One of the sons, Ham, made fun of Noah. The other two sons shielded him from shame and covered their father. Noah blesses these two. Ham though is cursed by Noah.

If you are reminded of the Noah story when you view this card, it is a reminder that mocking another is an insulting thing to do. Noah was a man of greatness. His story demonstrates that even such a person has weak moments. No one is to be mocked in their moments of weakness.

• Endymion was asleep naked on Mount Latmos. Artemis the Moon goddess saw him from heaven and was so taken with his beauty that she came down to earth and made love to him in his dream. Endymion enjoyed the experience in his dream so much that he asked his father Zeus to give him perpetual beauty, everlasting sleep, and immortality so that he could have the sexual dream with Artemis forever. Zeus granted his wish and legend has it that Artemis visits him nighty in his immortal dream state. Artemis has given birth to fifty daughters.

• If this story resonates with you, it speaks of your Peter Pan side, the desire to maintain bliss and to avoid responsibilities.

• Peter Abélard lived in France from 1079 to 1144. As a noble he was entitled to knighthood, but he declined the honor. He was the foremost intellectual of his time and became the Schoolmaster of the Paris Cathedral. His reputation for brilliance and for his penetrating logic was such that intellectuals widely predicted that he would enter the church and eventually be proclaimed Pope. Students from across Europe flocked to Paris to hear him. He is credited with being the spiritual founder of the University of Paris.

When Abélard was 38, he was asked by Fulbert, one of the canons of Notre Dame, to tutor his sixteen-year-old niece, Héloïse. Héloïse was herself very bright. Her uncle's ambition was to secure for her an advantageous marriage.

Héloïse and Peter became lovers. Pregnant, she fled Paris and eventually delivered a son which they named Astrolabe for the recently invented navigational instrument. Fulbert sent hoodlums to Abélard's quarters at night and they castrated him. Héloïse became a nun and Abélard spent several years in a monastery before he was reinstated to his teaching position.

• There are times when opposing forces in my life bring about change. Sometimes the change is positive, sometimes it is negative, and sometimes the change is both positive and negative.

Picture Card 58

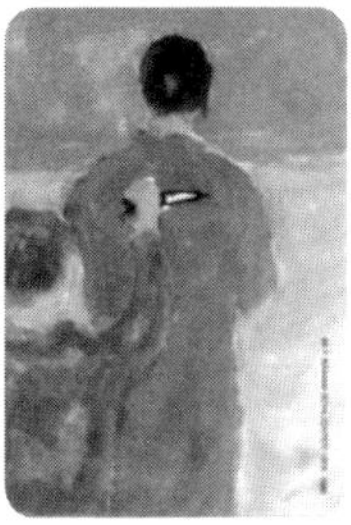

My back and my face are the two parts of my body which I cannot see. The vulnerability of my face is that it gives away my inner feelings and emotions. The vulnerability of my back is that it is exposed to a cowardly attack from another, usually someone I know. There is more danger from a friend than there is from an enemy because I keep my enemies at a distance. My friends have access to my feelings and emotions and are close enough to put an arm around my shoulder or a knife in my back. Friendship is the most important relationship there is among human beings. It is the one relationship where I am bonded to another, not by blood or by law, but rather by choice. What tears a friendship apart? By drawing this card I am indicating that harsh feelings exist towards a person who once was very close to me. When Abraham was ordered by God to sacrifice his son, Isaac, he chose a knife as the instrument of execution. Knives are employed often in initiations. They are the instruments used in circumcisions. Freudians see the knife as a phallic symbol. When Moses speaks of having seen God face to face or having seen God's back, he is speaking of the mystery of the divine presence within himself. To see myself face to face and see my own back means that I have risen above sense perception. I am now capable of unconditional love, a state in which no person can be an enemy.

• When someone makes unkind remarks about me behind my back, it affects me more deeply if my attacker is a friend. This card alerts me to my state of vulnerability.

• Romulus and Remus were twin brothers. When they were very young, they were thrown into the Tiber River by Amulius. The twins were miraculously washed ashore and succored by a she-wolf who fed them her milk. A shepherd found them and raised them as his sons. Later when the brothers were building Rome, they argued and Romulus killed Remus.

• Moses and his brother Aaron were the co-liberators of the Hebrew people who were enslaved in Egypt. Yet when Moses married an Ethiopian woman, Aaron rebelled against his brother. (*Numbers* 12:1) Being related by blood does not guarantee protection from an attack. Nor does the fact that the siblings shared all manner of dangers prevent them from turning against each other.

• Jesus once told a parable about a farmer whose newly seeded fields produced as many weeds as it did plants. (*Matthew* 13:25) The farmer mused that an enemy had planted weeds among his crops. Exactly who is my enemy? The enemy as archetype is certainly one of the most pervasive archetypes in the human experience. From childhood on I have been taught that enemies bring about evil. Early stories told me about a bad wolf, dangerous bears, an evil stepmother, even a vengeful piper. The masks I place on enemies are those of foreigners, barbarians, and strangers. Beneath these masks is a familiar visage, none other than my own. As complex as it is to grasp and as difficult as it is to accept, it is my own shadow material which manifests as my enemy.

Picture Card 59

This card symbolizes anything which is dual or two-sided in which both sides are equally at work. The brain is a good example of the symbolism in the card. The runner on the left signifies the left brain activity and the runner on the right signifies the right brain activity. In the West, we equate right and left with male and female or active and passive or day and night or extrovert and introvert. The right is the male, active, daytime, extrovert principle. The left is the female, passive, nighttime, introvert principle.

In the tradition of China and the Far East the tradition is reversed. For instance, yang is the male principle or left and yin is right and the female principle. Five is the number of balance and harmony while two is the number of confrontation and conflict. These elements, like right and left, are always in juxtaposition to each other. Within me, my right and my left, my male and my female, my active and my passive, and my fiveness and my twoness are my two sides. There is no reason for either side to dominate the other. Too much of one side stifles the other. The card asks me to keep my disparate parts harmonized.

Picture Card 60

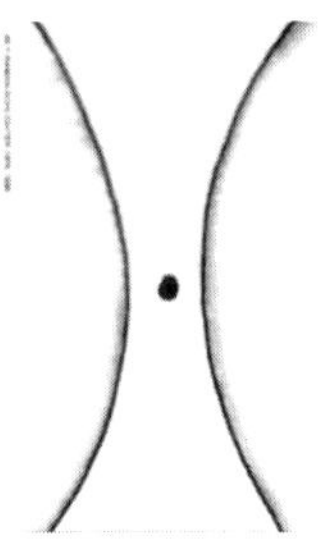

Graphic symbols are used worldwide to convey meanings; some are abstract and some are tangible. The sign pictured in this card is both. As a tangible sign, it is used in meteorological systems to mean that there is heavy precipitation and that the rain is far from the observation station. The dot stands for water and the backward parentheses are used to symbolize distance.

As an abstract sign, the image in this card is a rendition of a *yantra.* A yantra is a geometric figure which symbolizes manifestation of the cosmos and the power which brought it into existence. The figure itself is a prayer, a written equivalent of the mantra. The mantra is a phrase passed along from a teacher to a student who uses it in a ritual to achieve a oneness with the universe. With the mantra I vibrate with the cosmos and share its energy.

This card symbolizes the sacred communion I can achieve with the cosmos. The card masks its secret meanings. These I am able to understand when I animate the symbol in my own ritual. I concentrate on the dot. The yantra will enable me to move beyond the world of senses.

Picture Card 61

Twentieth century bathrooms were decorated with white tile whenever the owners could afford it. The whiteness and the tile both symbolize initiation. Tile symbolizes the protection of a secret. The word for white in Latin is *candidus*. Candidates for public office in Ancient Rome wore white as do candidates for baptism and certain initiatory rites. Here, though, the bathroom is mainly green, adding another dimension, that of regeneration. Many people view excrement with great dread, even their own. Yet it is endowed with great power. People relate excrement to the dark side. The maggot eats carrion and life is reborn. Excrement symbolizes the person who has few assets and yet is rich.

• People everywhere in all ages bathe. The bath is the primary ritual which marks entry into birth, puberty, and death. Immersion is like a return to the womb. That is why a hot bath feels so good. I feel soothed. At the same time, immersion is also a form of burial, entry into a state of oblivion, where I have no duties. Water cleanses and also fructifies, thus the ritual of immersing women after their menstrual cycle. Water symbolizes the regeneration process. Ritual washing is a form of purification.

• To draw this card means that I am seeking to be reborn. Some people put perfume or cologne on their bodies in direct proportion to how they feel about themselves. Excessive perfume or cologne means I do not think much of myself. I do not want to smell my own scent. The card says that I cannot become this new person through artificial means. Everything must be natural. Fear of my own odor is a belief of impotence. Acceptance of self is a sign of strength.

• I go to the bathroom to minister unto myself. I relieve myself at the toilet or bathe myself in running water. I am in need of self-care. I will turn within and let my soul be cleansed. While that which is green is seen as vigorous and full of life, it can also be that which is not ready or ripe such as green apples. Green is the name for a rookie. It is also the color of envy and of the unsophisticated. The green room is where I wait before making my grand appearance on television. The green light is my signal to go, to move out.

• David remained at his royal palace in Jerusalem after he sent his army to do battle with the enemy. One evening he was strolling on his roof when he saw a beautiful woman bathing in a nearby residence. Her name was Bathsheba, the wife of Uriah, one of David's soldiers. She became pregnant by David. Later in order to protect their illicit relationship, David sent Uriah into the worst of the fighting and Uriah was killed. (*II Samuel* 11:1-12:25)

If you remember the story of David and Bathsheba when you view the card, you are dealing with a question of betrayal which is unpunished at the moment.

Picture Card 62

The uniform. The badge. The whistle. The upraised arm. All these tell me to stop. The person in the uniform is transformed the instant the uniform is donned. A new title is conferred and a figure of authority is created.

I have within me a conscience which is my personal police officer. The function it plays is as governor of my actions. It slows me down or speeds me up. It tells me to come or advises me to go. In a contest the participants are guided by a whistle. The sound of the whistle halts play. It stops all the action. The hand in the air in the picture also halts the action. The card's advice is direct and to the point. Stop.

• A whistle is also the signal to start. That which is stop in one scenario is start in another.

Picture Card 63

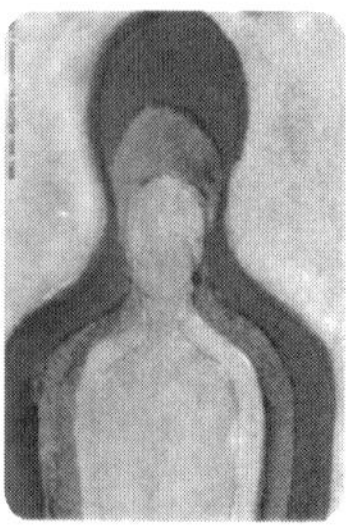

This card represents the arithmetical progression of the numbers One, Two, Three, and Four. I have several selves. My outer personality or *persona* has a life of its own. It dominates me. Yet my persona is something I created. I can change it if I choose. The same thing holds true for my inner personality, my *anima*. My anima is a reverse reflection of my persona. If my outer self shows itself as a strong, masculine figure, my inner self will be gentle and feminine. If I instill fear in others, my inner self will exhibit fear and foreboding.

• There are four figures pictured here. Spiritually, they represent the Divine Father, the Divine Mother, the Divine Child, and the Divine Love among them. The Divine Quaternity consists of the arithmetical progression of the numbers One, Two, Three, and Four.

• The quaternary number is a symbol of the cosmos and its perfection. Pythagoras called this concept the "tetraktys." The tetraktys contains the knowledge of all things. The tetraktys is a whole. I also am a whole. Like the tetraktys, all knowledge resides within me. All so-called mysteries or secrets of the universe are mine. To manifest it requires a discipline on my part. It will not come flashing into my life like a thunderbolt. There is no god to whom I can pray for this knowledge. I possess a sacred character. Living a profane life blocks expression of my sacred character. This card expresses the perfect number through which I can obtain knowledge of myself, knowledge of the Deity within me, and knowledge of all things which exist.

Picture Card 64

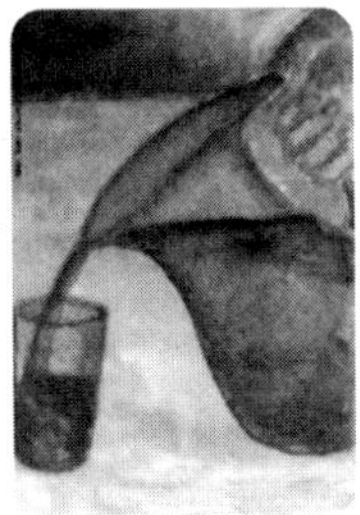

Question: How do I empty an ocean? Answer: One glass at a time. Water is the symbol of the undifferentiated. For the first 14 days of my existence I was an undifferentiated mass. As a zygot I had no parts, nor could I be called a whole since I could not be divided. I had no future and no past. The singularity of my conception signaled my beginning and yet there was no I. This is a state to which I aspire even now through meditation. I want to become lost in the infinity of the undifferentiated state. A glass of water dissolves once it returns to the ocean. It has gained a fresh strength from the vast resources of the potential. There is potential in the zygot. There is nothing to damn and nothing to praise. I live in the waters which have no shores. Primordial formlessness and nothingness mark me. I take these thoughts into my meditation.

Picture Card 65

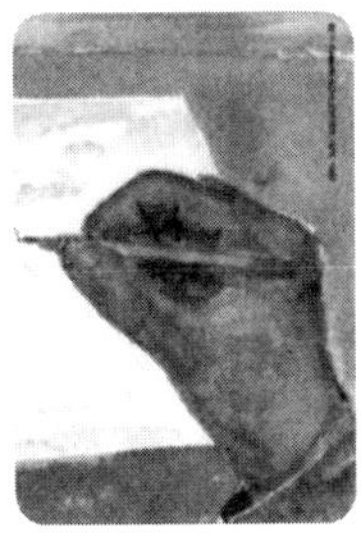

Speech and writing both involve words. Speech is the primary system of human communication. Writing exists only to take the place of speech. Writing is the physical manifestation of speech. It takes away the human aspect of speech and replaces it with signs. Most masters did not involve themselves with writing. Muhammad did not write. Nor did Pythagoras, Buddha, Socrates, or Jesus. People who write proselytize. They are looking for converts like Peter and Paul did or they are fixing rules for their members like Moses and the Prophets.

I cannot record anything on my soul with a pen. Speech is sound and thereby partakes of the infinite nature of sound. Some alphabets and methods of writing are symbols rather than signs. Early ideograms and hieroglyphics derive from ritual languages. Sanskrit letters derive from yantra, the written form of mantra.

• The card is a symbol of memorialization, keeping a record of what has transpired. It means writing my thoughts for myself as in a journal. The way I do my rituals, the way I meditate, the dreams I have, the way I pray should all be written in my daily *examen*. This way I can look back to see where I have been. In esotericism, whether Muslim or Judaic, letters are numbers. The numbers represent images and elements which then give a different meaning to the written words. Kabbalists interpret the Torah in this fashion. If my writing becomes sacred rather than profane or mundane it too will have hidden meanings.

• In the Islamic tradition, Allah created the Quill or Pen *(qalam)* from a precious substance in order to write upon the Tablet. On the Tablet Allah wrote about every event which will occur before the Resurrection. He is the only one who knows what is written on the Tablet. In the book *Chronicles*, Tabari wrote that the precious substance from which *qalam* was made was light and it was created a thousand years before anything else. In the allegory God says, "Write!" The Pen answers, "What shall I write?" "Fate!" God answers. The Pen has one split end so that light flows from it. The writing comes from the other end.

• When I am awakened by a dream and immediately record it in my journal before I forget it, I am writing with the light of my unconscious.

• Good authors who are suffering from a writer's block simply begin writing even if it is gibberish. Gradually the right words will find the way from the pen to the paper.

• Reminiscent of the allegory of the *qalam*, John begins his Gospel with, "In the beginning was the Word, and the Word was with God, and the Word was God. He was in the beginning with God. All things came into being by Him, and apart from Him nothing came into being that has come into being. In Him was life, and the life was the light of men. And the light shines in the darkness, and the darkness did not comprehend it." *John* 1:1-5.

Picture Card 66

All primitive societies have an initiation process for youths to pass from adolescence to manhood. Most of these rituals test the youth's courage, their bravery, intuitive skills, and the ability to deal with a crisis. Only Judaism created a rite of passage related to literacy. In *Deuteronomy* 31:10-11, God mandated that every Jew had to learn to read and to teach the children to read. Modern Judaism requires the girl or boy candidates for Bar or Bat Mitzvah to master a Torah portion and to deliver a sermon about it to the assembled congregation.

• A book is the symbol of knowledge, wisdom, and the truth. The truth cannot be put in a book any more than it can be bottled. Nor can knowledge. Nor can wisdom. Yet it is to a book I go when I seek these. At a deeper level a book symbolizes the cosmos. The cosmos is closed and yet it expands, faster now than when it originated. The letters in the book represent human beings and everything else in the universe. The words which are formed from the letters represent the events which occur throughout the universe. Within the book of the cosmos, all events are represented. They occur, pass away, and then occur again over and over. Since all events are within the book, the book becomes revelation and manifestation. In other words, I can know all things, become wise through such knowledge, and observe the truth as it manifests. There are books of such revelation, some extant, some no longer here. Witness the Koran, the Bible, Torah, and the Book of Mormon. These came to be such because they present in intelligible form the same universal message. Yet there are more such books, one in particular which is more suited for me. That book is the one which I craft for myself. There is no need to look beyond my own inner book for the masterpiece I seek. The Master is I, abiding within me and directing my every move. It is my own patterning forever guiding me and providing me with cosmic intelligence.

Picture Card 67

Dance is natural for all living things. It is more than anything a wonderful language which is beyond words. Birds, grasshoppers, and bees dance to express their urges with a feverish style which approaches frenzy. Dance does much more than words can ever do, for dance tells the story of life. If words tried to tell such a story, they would be unintelligible.

• Dance throws off all sense of temporality and physicality. My body and my soul merge, visible becomes invisible and suddenly I am lost in ecstasy. When Mawlana, founder of the Dervishes, did his dance, everyone could see that he was caught up in rapture. It is the same with David when he dances naked as he entered Jerusalem before the Ark of the Covenant. These are primary dances, those which are sacred. The sacred dance has a mystical ascension. It is as if I am climbing a ladder. The arrangement and the rhythm of the dance, especially with drums, afford me the opportunity to escape all sense of being earthbound.

• All mystery religions practiced the dance as did the early Christians. Native Americans, Ancient Chinese, and Greeks recognized the importance of the dance in walking the path of invisibility. The card is inviting me to bring my body into my quest to reach the spiritual state. The aesthetic, the emotional, the erotic, the physical, and the spiritual become one when I fuse them into my dance. In Chinese tradition it is Number which keeps the universe functioning, from the stars and planets to the ants and archetypes. The dance is a rhythm of Number and it creates the harmony of heaven and Earth. It will do no less for me.

• The dance creates a patterned design through space which the observer can trace visually. The dance is performed in measured units of time. When I as the dancer move my body in accordance with the music's temperament with measured steps, my rhythmic movements draw the praise of others.

• It is another story altogether when I dance to a tune different from others.

• Dance is an expression of joy.

• Companionship is essential to fulfillment in life. When my desire for companionship is platonic rather than sexual or homosexual rather than heterosexual, it simply means that I have no need to have a traditional family. My relationships in my profession or other work are quite satisfying.

Picture Card 68

Tension and stress have brought me to the point of total withdrawal. Lethargy is a natural result of withdrawal. I have the feeling that there is no answer to the problem I am facing or to the grief with which I am dealing. If I examine all the times in my life when I have had difficulty I will find that there is one central person at the center of each scenario. That person is me. Rather than focusing on my depression, I focus on the role I have been playing and my manner in acting out my role. This is no easy task because the issues and questions I am raising bear no relationship to the real problem. In order to bring about change I must literally be the change. A problem is never solved at the level of the problem. A solution to any problem begins with self-analysis.

• People do not gravitate toward me. I do not have the sparkle which would attract others to me. I do not aspire to renown. The memories of childhood miseries plague me. I find no release from inner frustrations.

Picture Card 69

I compare this card with Number 17, the three figures. What differences do I note? None of the five figures is moving or walking. Or are they on a magic carpet which transports them past life's experiences and events. I look at the picture and let my mind turn around until another image appears. Two is the symbol of conflict which underlies all activity. Seen as pairs of extremes, two produces balance. Seen as pairs of opposites, they pose a threat one to the other. Two is ambivalence, never able to make up its mind. Two is the split, the rivalry, the duality. Think of the yin and yang, the male and the female. It can be a push, antagonistic, or a pull, attracting. I look at the colors the figures are wearing. I observe the pattern of their dress. I look at the object on the left. Now I speak the picture which comes to my mind.

Picture Card 70

Planting contains several hidden processes. To the uninitiated it appears miraculous that a seed placed in soil produces a living object which grows into a thing of beauty, thrives for its lifetime, and then fades away into nothingness. Plant life is green, which reflects its regenerative process. Its upper body sucks in fire, the Sun's energy; its roots suck in the water, its bloodstream; it also sucks in air from which it withdraws oxygen and it gets its vitamins from the soil. The plant is the manifestation of the Sun's energy and the water from which it never separates. The driest cactus is filled with water. In the Koran it says, "God made me to grow from the earth like a plant." There is an underlying unity of all life and I am the same as that which is planted. I have the same cycle of the plant – birth, growth, death, and transfiguration.

This card brings to mind these cycles and asks me to celebrate my birth, my growth, even my death which signals my movement into the transcendent. Just as the farmer is doing in the card, I must continue this process no matter what I am doing. When I plant flowers in my garden, if they do not come up I never blame the flowers. I might blame the lack of sunshine, the wrong fertilizer, or too much water. But I never blame the flowers. Yet when I have a conflict with a parent or a spouse or a relative or a friend, I blame the other person. The card invites me to remove the sense of blame from my thinking and substitute love and understanding. Every relationship I have is a planting. If you have $10.00 and I have $10.00 and you give me yours and I give you mine, we each will have the same $10.00. On the other hand, if I give you my idea and you give me yours, we each have two ideas instead of one. I plant ideas in others, nurture them, and help them grow. I put aside those things which have completed their cycles and I enable others by sharing my transcendent self.

• Each of us sows our own seed. When some sow religion, there will automatically be others who will sow heresy. When some sow antagonism, there will arise others to sow peace and respect for others. Just as the farmer scatters seed in order that it may grow, I sow seed with every word I speak, with my thinking, and with my actions. What I do not realize when I sow is that what I sow will one day be my sustenance. You may call it karma or retribution. Nevertheless it is a rule of nature that what I sow, I will reap.

• Each seed contains within it a life which will come into being and make a contribution to nature whether as a twig, a thorn, or an ear of corn. Similarly with my words, my thoughts, and my actions: Each is a life. Each makes a contribution, whether plus or minus.

• That which the farmer sows will grow where once a forest flourished. The farmer now controls what will grow there. In a storm the plants will bow down. When the storm is over the plants will rise up again. The plants will all be sown and harvested at the same time, symbolic of the death of all. Theirs is more reminiscent of many men dying together, as in a battle. As the farmer plants the seeds he knows that they will bear fruit many, many times over, perhaps a hundredfold.

• Though it is performed by both men and women, horticulture is basically a feminine activity. The seed is carefully placed in the earth, covered, and nurtured until it blooms and delivers more seeds or fruit.

Picture Card 71

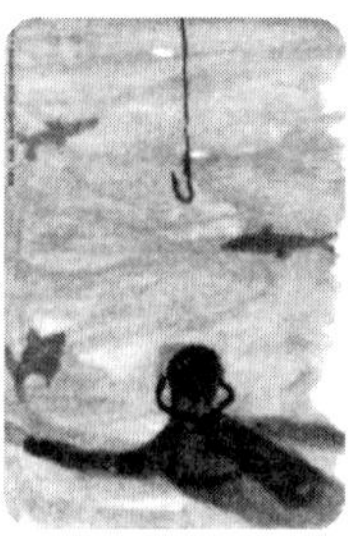

Jules Verne ran away from home and went to sea at the age of eleven. When the ship reached its first port, he returned home. He promised his mother that in the future he would travel only in his imagination. He wrote 60 adventure novels. He anticipated the submarine in *Twenty Thousands Leagues Under the Sea*. In other novels he anticipated the light bulb, the electric clock, and space travel. This card allows me to put myself into the darkness of the sea and experience it from the point of view of the dwellers of another realm.

• *Leviticus* is the section of the Old Testament which fixes Judaic dietary laws. Of all the aquatic creatures the only ones which are allowed to be eaten are fish. The proscription against sea dwellers even extends to some of the fish. Only those with gills and without scales may be eaten. The early Christians used the Greek word for fish *(ichthus)* as an ideogram. The Greek initials stand for *Iesu Christos Theou Uios Soter (Jesus Christ, Son of God, Savior).* They scratched pictures of fish on doors and posts at the entrance to their homes as signals to each other. In *Luke* 24:42, the story is told of Jesus eating fish after his resurrection. Fish became a symbol of the Eucharist.

• In Ancient Egypt fish was part of the daily diet. However, neither the priests nor the Pharaoh were allowed to eat fish because it was believed that certain gods turned themselves into fish. Fish lay huge numbers of eggs and have come to symbolize fertility and life itself. Perhaps for this reason, Leviticus forbade the use of fish in sacrifices. As I swim in the depths of the water I can see very little. It is quite dark. Yet though it is very dark I can sense that there is life around me. I cannot see its form or shape. I cannot touch it or hear it. This is the way my unconscious works. I am swimming around in my deep unconscious. Life abounds around me. The creatures around me are like messengers bringing me information and knowledge through my dreams or my oracle. I reach out and there is nothing there.

Roaming through the deep waters of the unconscious is not without peril. There are dangers lurking in the darkness. Some who venture into the deep never return from the depths. Some come back permanently scarred. Others though come back whole. The card symbolizes the abundance and the mystery afforded by my unconscious. The hook symbolizes the process of abstracting elements from my unconscious. In fishing there is no use for logic. There is no accurate way to predict the result of my effort. The card reminds me to be spontaneous and receptive to messages from the unconscious and to use the OH Cards whenever the need arises and no matter wherever I happen to be. I am receptive by agreeing in advance to use my oracle so that its energies will work within me and draw from my unconscious the advice or answer I need.

• A fish can live out of water about as long as I can live under the water without air. The diver in the card has overcome this anomaly by having air pumped through tanks. When I enter a hostile environment I must bring with me my means of survival.

• When a person is called a shark it means that the person is voracious and has predatory habits. The human shark enriches himself by taking advantage of others. It is interesting that the fish known as shark was given its name by German sailors from the word *Schurke,* a word applied to a person who was "a greedy parasite" – a scoundrel or villain. The word found its way among sailors of other nationalities and it entered the English vocabulary in 1569 when English sailors introduced the term as "shark." If you are called a shark you are a dangerous person who takes advantage of others – loan shark, card shark, gun shark.

Picture Card 72

This card through its image of the nurse is a symbol of dedication. How the nurse is dressed reflects her stages of training – the apron, the nursing cap, the band on the cap, the white uniform, and finally the pin which marks the nurse as a trained professional. The nurse follows the doctor's orders for treating the patient and contributes the healing care and touch needed in executing them. The patient's needs are considered greater than her own.

Picture Card 73

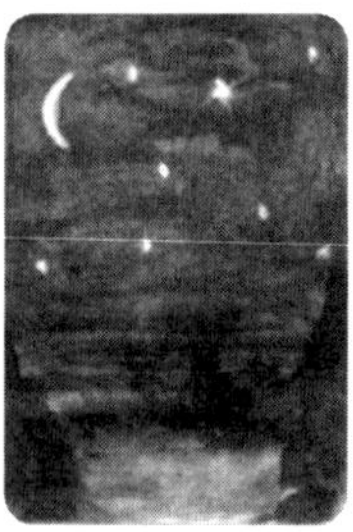

According to the Ancient Greeks, night is the daughter of Chaos. It brings suffering to those confined to a sickbed and pathos to those incarcerated in jail. In the darkness of sleep, the unconscious roams free, unimpeded by logic or desires. Conspiracy, crime, and danger flourish in the dark hours.

• There is light even at night. The stars you see painted on the ceilings of churches and temples symbolize that the light the stars furnish is of divine origin. They are symbols of the spiritual forces which guide me through the dark moments of my life. The moon as depicted waxes and wanes. It symbolizes dependence since it has no light of its own. It also symbolizes periodic change and, as a crescent, it signifies growth.

• Night is the symbol of gestation, the seed in the ground, the fetus in the womb, the product of which will appear in the daylight. Night is the time when roots grow.

The presence of light in the darkened night sky portrays the passing and temporal nature of all things. Relief always appears with the dawn. Things always look better in the light of day. In Judaism, night begins each day.

Picture Card 74

This card pictures the symbol of physical nourishment, which is the food I eat every day and of spiritual nourishment, which is the food for my soul. It also pictures shakers of salt and pepper, which are condiments I add to flavor my food and which also have symbolic meanings. The Second Law of Thermodynamics says that if I mix the salt with the pepper they can never be separated again into salt and pepper. Once mixed, they stay mixed. One of the better known Tantric symbols is of one grain of salt in a glass of water which symbolizes the reintegration of the Ego into the Universal Being.

• Catholics believe that those who hunger for righteousness receive the sacred bread of eternal life. Bread is very much a part of the ritual of the Catholic Mass. Shew Bread was maintained in the Ark of the Covenant signifying the symbolic presence of God in the physical presence of bread.

• This card symbolizes appetite. There is but one appetite. It is not an appetite for food or sex or money. It is an appetite for the Transcendent, for Communion with God. Desires for food or sex are false appetites. After the third day without food a faster no longer craves food. Those who take a vow of chastity disdain involvement with sex. Those who take a vow of poverty disdain money.

Europeans and Asians coming to America for the first time and seeing so many overweight people feel like they are visiting a fat farm. Americans are the fattest people in the history of the world. In the United States people look for large portions and shovel their food in rather than savoring it. Americans are obsessed with weight and they do not lose it. The same applies to sex and to money. People are yielding to communal temptations. The message of the card says that I should look to my true appetite, the Transcendent. What is my favorite food? Praise? How do I nourish and develop my inner being?

Picture Card 75

This card represents another of the universal symbols pictured in the OH Cards. The symbol of a crossroads is known in all cultures through all ages. It is a place of mystery and magic, and it was where ancient peoples performed many different rituals. One such was to leave a stone at the crossroads. Over the years these would accumulate and a mound or a pyramid would rise. Out of this grew the sense that a crossroads is the center of the world.

• In the card one aspect of me is headed east following the red arrow. This represents birth or rebirth. The other part of me is headed south, as represented by the black arrow, towards the place which lies on the Sun's left hand, the place of thorns.

• The crossroads is a place of revelation. I am being instructed to examine the struggle within me which is tugging me in disparate directions. Do I want to commit myself to the process of rebirth, or do I want to abandon the process in favor of a life spent in the world of senses. Perhaps it is better just to work in my garden than it is to uncover and discover my real identity. The Latin word for crossroads illustrates this dichotomy. It is *trivium* which happens also to be the root word for *trivial.* One of the choices at a crossroads is to seek the trivial in life. The choice is mine to determine.

Picture Card 76

The hearth is the core symbol of the home and the union of lovers, man/man, man/woman, and woman/woman and the center of life. People gather round the hearth for social intercourse; food can be cooked there. The hearth can be a shrine where prayers are said, rituals are observed, and sacred statues are kept.

There are five tongues of flames in the hearth. These are symbolic of the vital energy points in my spiritual body. Buddha used the symbolism of fire as the energy within a person which enables knowledge and enlightenment to thrive and the outer shell to disappear. "I kindle the flame within myself," the Buddha said, "My heart is the hearth, the flame is the taming of self." Other teachers also use the system of symbolically flaming each of the chakras. The tongues of fire are reminiscent of the promise of Jesus to send the Holy Spirit to his Apostles. I stare into the flames in the hearth and let myself become transported. The flames purify and regenerate. I am seeking understanding within my spirit and I will find it. The animal figurines on the mantle, the tortoise and the hare, ask me to determine my speed – fast or slow.

• A fireplace cannot function without a chimney. That which is within always manifests in the outer. My inner fire will always be known by everyone.

• Fire is the same always and everywhere. However it starts and for however long it lasts, fire always retains the same image. It is very contagious and spreads rapidly. Everything in its path disappears into the air. To keep a fire going in a hearth I have to keep feeding the fire or it will die.

The symbolism of the fire is that it needs new converts who are willing to give themselves wholly to the cause. If I have an idea which will die unless it has believers who are willing to be swallowed up and lose their identities for the idea, the idea is not worth having. An idea which is the truth does not need followers. It spreads without effort.

• Fire is violent. When it is in my hearth I have contained the violence. Whenever I stand at a fire such as at a bonfire or at a fireplace, I have the urge to urinate. This may be my inner urge to produce water in order to put the fire out. Fire makes fear. People panic and run away from fire. This fear dissipates when fire is in the hearth. For me then, fire can mean that an aspect of my patterning is to become a human fire extinguisher, to be a person who settles disputes or who, in the vernacular, puts out fires. I determine my patterning by looking to my explanation and definition of symbols.

Picture Card 77

As Judas hugged Jesus, Jesus asked him whether he would betray him with a kiss. As Caesar sees Brutus approaching with a knife, he asks, "How could you do this, Brutus?" Each party is embracing the other with but one arm only. A kiss is the coming together of two spirits. This is why the mouth is used. Breath is inhaled and exhaled through the mouth. When I kiss another I am breathing my spirit upon the other. When I kiss I am sending my soul to unify with another. In *Romans* 16:16, St. Paul exhorts his followers to salute each other with a holy kiss. The card advises that when I hug or kiss another or when I embrace an inner aspect of myself I must do it with holiness. An obstacle within myself must be embraced. It must be kissed. "I must leap into it," as Carlos Castenada says.

Picture Card 78

Tradition has it that 5000 years ago the symbolism of the trigram was revealed to Fu Hsi through markings on the shell of a turtle. There are eight trigrams, consisting of straight lines (yang) and broken lines (yin), which form the 64 hexagrams of the I Ching. The *I Ching* or *Book of Changes* was the only book to escape burning when Ch'in Shih Huang

Ti in the third century BCC ordered the burning of all books of philosophy.

The turtle has come to represent a whole cosmography. The upper half of its shell is curved like the heavens. The lower half is flat like the Earth. In several cultures, the creation myth centers around a turtle upon whose back the earth or the entire universe is supported. The turtle has a lengthy life span and this has fostered symbolism related to longevity and eternity.

Modern Chinese has several metaphors with sexual overtones related to the turtle. For instance, both the cuckhold husband and the pimp are called turtle because they ignore the intercourse their women engage in. The turtle's head out is metaphorically related to the erect penis and the reverse refers to the soft penis. Meditation is a withdrawing much like the ostrich in the sand or the turtle going within its shell. The deeper symbolism of the turtle is that of protection. This card symbolizes that whenever I am in danger I have the means with which to protect myself.

Picture Card 79

The general notion is that each individual enters life at birth with a *tabula rasa*, a clean slate. The common belief is that I entered this life's experience blank and through events and relationships I fill the slate and then I die.

However, enlightened thinking holds that this belief is in error. Rather, the contrary is correct, which is that my slate was completely filled with my total patterning at the time I was conceived. Nothing was left out. My drives, desires, appetites, tendencies, character traits and behavioral patterns were all on the slate. A parallel exists within my physical being. A map of my DNA demonstrates that everything about me is already written, even down to the diseases I will contract, and manifests upon my conception.

• The card pictures the *tabula rasa* and the earthly teachers such as my ministers, parents, school teachers, authority figures and those commonly held beliefs which combine to fill my slate with false data. The teacher is elevated to symbolize that I receive my data from a higher authority. By pulling this card I have been given the realization that my guide in life is my inner teacher. To understand myself I must first understand my patterning. It is there waiting for me to uncover it.

Picture Card 80

This is a perfect card to teach me how to let my mind do a flip. The card depicts a man and a child. With this sight I can go only so far. I visualize instead that these are two adults, except that one is a dwarf. The dwarf symbolizes the dark side and represents the uncontrolled expressions of the unconscious. The dwarf is irresponsible, profane and speaks the unwelcome truth. Mostly the dwarf is mischievous and illogical. His remarks deflate everyone. I will treat the dwarf as my guide, my guardian. When I want to draw some strength from within, I will visualize my dwarf. I give myself an inner irreverent little person who will show me my spiritual pot of gold. The buried treasure is within me, as are the inner secrets I keep even from myself.

Picture Card 81

The secret to analyzing the image in this card is the seal above the judges. It is the symbol of their power and authority. In the picture the seal is not presented in its entirety. The rounded bottom is draped with a gold banner and the content of the message of the seal is hidden.

In the Old Testament, the instructions from God are under Seal. Daniel is told to seal his book (*Daniel* 12:4). The act of circumcision is a seal, initiating newborns into Judaism, whereas baptism is the seal for Christians. Once I am under the secret seal I am subject to its authority. The authority of the seal in the picture is exercised by a three-judge tribunal. It has three judges to show that it is divinely ordained, that its authority is suprahuman, and by its threeness, that it is complete. The card reminds me that in an ordered society there is an authority which governs us all. Likewise in my personal existence there is an authority governing me.

• A court is the residence of a sovereign. We no longer have a sovereign, yet our law assembly places are called "courts," where a judge or ruling authority (like a king) sits on an elevated platform (like a throne) and is attired in a robe (like a royal robe).

Picture Card 82

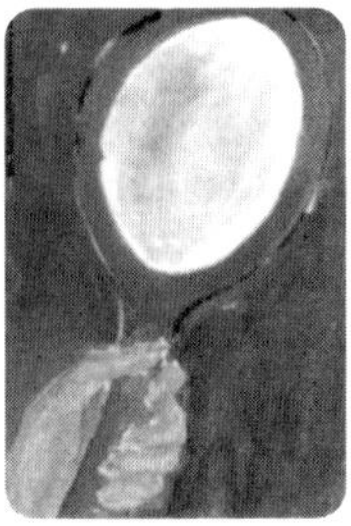

The Latin word for *mirror* is *speculum*. From this word we get the word *speculate*. To speculate means to reach a conclusion based upon whatever information is at hand. It also originally meant scanning the sky and observing the stars. The Latin word for star is *sidus* from which we get the word *consideration* which means to scan all the stars at once. Mirror, the tool for viewing the stars, symbolizes the truth and the purity which comes with it. A mirror symbolizes staying together; a broken mirror symbolizes separation.

Pythagoras made use of the mirror as an oracle by turning it towards the Moon and reading the future in it. Water surfaces are the same as mirrors and are used for divination. Chalk dust is sprinkled on the water and the patterns which emerge are then read. I, like a mirror, reflect beauty or ugliness. It is my soul which shows forth my true essence.

Self-knowledge is frightening, sometimes terrifying. Thus it can be said that the mirror is the symbol of symbolism. There are two sides of the mirror, the dull side and the polished side. My physical side is represented by the dull side, my soul by the polished side. To draw this card means that there has to be a careful examination of my habits and the way I am living. If I conclude that I like what I see, I am witnessing beauty. It is my essence. My face has never been seen directly by me. It can only be examined by me with the help of a mirror. In like fashion, my soul cannot be seen directly. It can only be examined with the help of a mystical mirror. The OH Cards are such an oracle.

• In Jewish tradition there are on the Earth at any given time 36 righteous persons who keep the universe functioning. They are called the *lamed vav*, Hebrew words for the *thirty and six*. These people never become famous for their righteousness. Rather, they perform their everyday tasks, putting everything in place, doing things in moderation, and maintaining a oneness within themselves. They are referred to in *Proverbs* 10:25: "The righteous is an everlasting foundation."

The righteous persons symbolize human perfection by creating order, first within themselves and then to everything around them. Together the *lamed vav* are a cosmic force. While *Proverbs* calls them foundations, they are often seen as the columns of the universe. The Talmud says that were there only one righteous person upon the face of the Earth, he or she would sustain the world.

This card asks me whether I will aspire to become a righteous person.

• This card also has the appearance of a frying pan. My pancake batter is ready for cooking. My sausage and eggs are also going to be cooked. The skillet is white hot. It sizzles. The hot skillet is the symbol for the process of nurturing others. I am the one upon whom others depend. I must live up to my duty.

• Is a period of revelry about to give way to a period of austerity? Pancake Day is a tradition celebrated on Shrove Tuesday before Ash Wednesday and the start of Lenten season of fasting. Ingredients are eggs symbolizing creation, flour symbolizing the staff of life, and salt symbolizing wholesomeness, and milk, symbolizing purity.

• Seen as a tennis racket, this card symbolizes friendly competition. Games release energy and relieve tension.

Picture Card 83

The handle and the scoop mean that the spade is suited for digging in the soil or moving the snow. Both functions are metaphors which involve the same type of action and which have quite different purposes. To "dig up the dirt" on someone means to seek to find scandal about another. On the other hand, the removal of snow is an act of loving-kindness. I am preparing a safe passage for another, unknown person.

• The card asks me how will I use my spade. Will I speak ill of another or will I perform acts of good works anonymously? The spade is also used in burials. Will I bury my feelings of ill will which I harbor towards another? Another view is that the spade can be used in cultivation. Cultivation means caring for and nurturing a relationship whether with plants or with people.

Picture Card 84

The bum and the monk each lead a live of poverty, devoid of material acquisitions, and dependent upon the charity of others. But society sees the bum as depraved and the monk as devout. It is a judgment call between good and evil.

• The bum is liberated from all social attributes and never has to qualify for anything. Nevertheless here is wisdom. This card signifies that I am polyvalent. It also is dealing with the me at my elemental level.

• The bum is holding out his left hand. The term *bumming* stems from the ritual of the hobo begging for money. The bum is to be distinguished from the beggar whose sole activity is to sponge off another. The bum is busily occupied, travels at will, and accepts no responsibilities. At the same time, the bum maintains an air of self-sufficiency if not downright superiority over everyone else. We admire the bum because of his freedom. We want to be like him, becoming as an example a golf bum or a tennis bum.

• The bum demonstrates that there is no need to struggle for supply. What he desires for today will appear, perhaps not when he asks for it but generally right on time to prevent disaster. The card refers to a time in life when I need to hear the message: "Calm down. Rest easy. Help is on the way." The power of the bum is in this realization.

• Excessive worry over money will minimize my ability to increase my earning potential. Fear begins as groundless worry. Worry generates an inability to compete and I wind up on the short end of the stick.

Picture Card 85

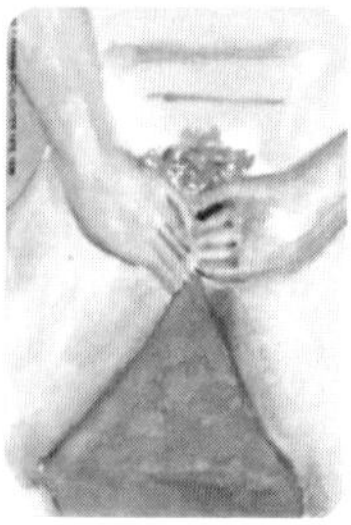

Some creation myths depict a ritual marriage of Heaven and Earth. An example of one such myth comes from the Dogon and Bambara people of Mali, who like all indigenous people fashioned stories about how the universe came to be created. The Earth's sexual organ was an anthill. As the creation process nears an end the anthill becomes a mouth or vulva out of which come the art of communication and the art of weaving which the ants taught to men. The vulva is the symbol of the way and the entry to secret wealth and hidden knowledge.

• The taking and giving process of the vulva is like the mouth eating food and regurgitating it in another form. The vulva swallows the penis and regurgitates life. The transmutation by the vulva is its mystery and its attraction. The vulva is said to be strong and not strong at the same time. The toothed vagina is the secret fear-fantasy of men. It fascinates a man to enter this place of mystery, opening to the possibility of life or even to death. This card symbolizes the development of my ability to fantasize. I have to feed fantasy in order to develop my dreams.

• The genitals represent maturity in psychosexual development. Oral and anal impulses become subordinated to those interpersonal mechanisms to which I adapt.

Picture Card 86

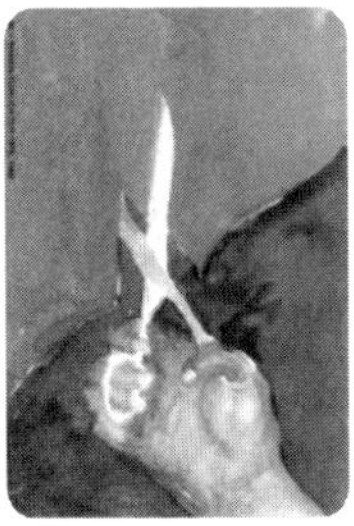

Red is the color of fire and blood and thereby derives its universal symbolization of the principle of life. Red signifies power, the strongest of energies. Bright red, like the blood which flows from a cut, signifies activity. It is a stimulating, life-embellishing symbol. Dark blood, on the other hand, has been stagnating within the body. By the time I see it its life-force has gone. Bright red is male. Dark red is female.

Blue, unlike red, rarely occurs in nature. I see it in the sky which is really a void; it is translucent, empty. While red is warm and full of life, blue is cold. Yet blue has a magical quality. Blue swallows up that which it encounters, much like infinity.

When blue and red are placed together as in this card they represent a coming together of Heaven and Earth. Scissors represent the cutting of the thread of life. The card therefore symbolizes the possibility of a major change. When I have asked whether a certain course of conduct should be followed, the card means it would be cutting out my heart to follow it.

• Cloth is made by weaving together natural or synthetic fibers. It is a union of such permanency that it takes force or sharp objects like scissors to tear or cut it apart.

• The worst insult I can give another is called the "unkindest cut of all." It is the worst treachery imaginable. The words come from Shakespeare's description of the stabbing of Julius Caesar by his friends. (*Julius Caesar* 3:2).

• Alexander the Great became the ruler of Asia because he cut the Gordian knot instead of trying to untie it.

• When projects are bound up in dead-end rules, the solution is to cut through the red tape. Red is the color of the string used to tie up legal documents which dates back to the 17th century in England.

Picture Card 87

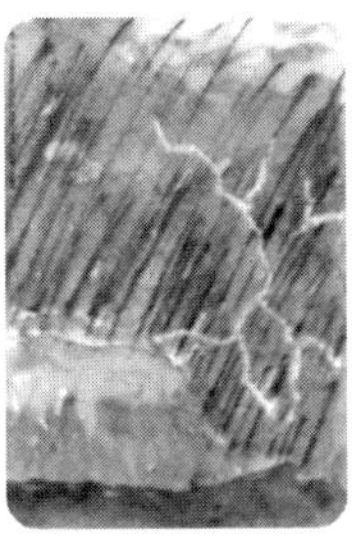

This card has two significant symbolic meanings. A person who relishes storms, or likes to walk through driving rains, or is excited by violent weather is a person who is intense and driven to do the unusual. For such a person there is no task too difficult, no mountain too high, and no thrill too bizarre. The storm lover goes through life swept along by passion and emotion. If this describes me, it means that I am creating a new adventure, one that will shake up those around me.

• Another meaning is for the person who sees God's hand in everything. The raging of the storm is the Voice of God, angry and outraged at the sinful actions of human beings. For this person the storm is frightening and bewildering. There is a force at work which brings suffering for the wrong committed. If this describes me, I must consider working to lessen my reliance on exterior forces.

• When the wind is powerful, its voice is loud. One says that the wind is howling when it is at its strongest. Wind is named by the direction from which it comes. When I feel the wind it is as though I am being touched by an entity which is alive. Even though the wind cannot be seen, its effects can be seen. Leaves flutter. Dust swirls. The wind makes a flag come alive. When wind is accompanied by rain and lightning as it is shown in this card, the storm is frightening. The wind may shriek like a warning siren. Normally, my voice is modulated but sometimes it is loud and threatening like the howling wind.

• Even though rain falls in individual drops, it is customarily seen as a singular unit. At times we need rain and pray for it or perform dances for it. At other times too much of it comes and flood results. Rain's flow is downward. It is always falling. Falling is something I try to avoid. In the card the rain is falling very hard. The darkness is penetrated by the lightning which adds to my sense of danger in the storm. The water below is turbulent. It is hardly a good time for sailing.

• The universe is made up of pairs of extremes. Looking at this card and seeing the light through the darkness are acknowledgments of this principle. Light did not appear in our cosmos until a billion years after the Big Bang. Yet it was always there. Night cannot exist without day. Illness cannot exist without well-being. Their union is the harmony of health. There is no such thing as good health or bad health, only health. This card is a reminder of the creation process, the comng together of the pairs of extremes.

• Hero was a beautiful princess of Aphrodite. At a festival held at Sestus, Leander saw her and fell madly in love with her. Afterwards Hero placed a torch in her tower and Leander would swim the Hellespont, a narrow strait between Asia and Europe, guided by the light from the tower just to be with her. One stormy might the light from the tower could not be seen but Leander tried to swim across the strait in spite of the obvious danger and he drowned. The next day Hero discovered his dead body which had washed ashore at Sestus. Overcome by grief, Hero drowned herself. The story of Hero and Leander has been told and retold by Shakespeare, Marlowe, Bryon, Keats, Tennyson, Cowley, Hood, Nash, and others.

Picture Card 88

The clown is the reverse image of a king and thus has come to be the symbol of the king who has been murdered. A king speaks in a proper way, stands, and walks in an auspicious way. A clown acts in the exact opposite manner. A clown is irreverent. A king is majestic. A clown does not recognize authority. A king is the authority. People are in awe of the king. A clown is in awe of nothing. Laughter is the clown's awe. A king has royal ceremonies. A clown ridicules everything sacred. To draw this card means that I am not taking things very seriously. I am relegating my inner king to a backseat while my less formal self holds sway.

• The grotesque make-up of the clown is meant to reflect his coarse interior. Do I truly reflect my inner self?

• The clown has a manner which causes us not to take things so seriously, especially ourselves. Laughter is the best medicine for all ills plus it is the most subtle way to overcome reality.

PART III

Word Card 89

AFFECTION

For Pythagoras, the most enduring relationship between two human beings is friendship. Since numbers constituted for Pythagoras the most valid method of communication, he defined the affection of friendship with a pair of numbers, 220 and 284. The divisors of 220 are 1, 2, 4, 5, 10, 11, 20, 22, 44, 55, and 110. They add up to 284. The divisors of 284 are 1, 2, 4, 71, and 142. They add up to 220. Pythagoras interpreted this anomaly as meaning that at heart 284 and 220 were each other. Affection is like this. When I feel affection for another and that person feels affection for me, ours is the most sincere of all relationships, friendship. I feel what my friend feels and my friend feels what I feel. We say the affection is mutual.

• Pythagoras called numbers such as 220 and 284 numbers of friendship and affection. He taught that there are an infinity of such numbers. About a hundred such couples have been discovered to date.

• This is an action card. Someone is influencing another, moving somebody's mind in a particular way. The card represents my feeling, my disposition, my emotion, or my passion toward a person or thing which I strongly want to affect. Affection for another is concern, solicitude, tenderness, warmth, and loyalty. If I have coolness, detachment, or antipathy, I cannot be a friend.

• It is often overlooked that children have the same need for affection as adults. The need in a child for loving care rivals in intensity the same need in an adult.

Word Card 90

ALONE

The word *alone* is a coming together of the words *all* and *one*. It means having no equal, serving as the sole example, being the record holder, or sacrificing one's self as the martyr to a cause. As a concept it can also mean that there is no one else in the same situation or predicament. Here it could also mean that I am single and separate from another whom I would like to have as a companion. Whether I remain friendless and solitary will depend a great deal upon my attitude.

• I must remember that I am unique. There are times when privacy is a priority for me. When I want to spend time examining concepts, working through problems, or closely looking at all of the facts, I want to be alone. This is particularly true when I am called upon to make a presentation. Before experiencing something new, I make a point of looking at it conceptually during a period of solitude.

• When I have to go it alone, it means that I have an arduous task and no one except me can do it.

Word Card 91

ANGER

Satchel Paige, the great baseball player, warned against fried foods: They make the blood boil. He said anger is a boiling, that which brings pain. When I express anger, I am boiling. That is why friends tell me to keep my cool when I become angry. A bad cut is called an angry wound. Rage and wrath are directed to the person or situation which causes the distress. Many times anger results from my own childish petulance. If I did not get my way or if someone has irritated me because of what they did or said, my anger is probably self-directed. I must remember that every expression is self-directed. My indignation is my indignation, not someone else's. I will live by the axiom that I will never let anything bother me or drive me to anger.

• In *Numbers* 22, there is a story about a man named Balaam who possessed the power to bless and the power to curse. When the Hebrews, newly liberated from Egypt, were across the Jordan and about to pass through Moab, the King of Moab, Balak, asked Balaam to put a curse on the invaders. Balaam consulted his oracle and he was advised not to curse the Hebrews because they were blessed. Balak persisted and sent a delegation for Balaam. Balaam saddled his donkey and rode off to lay the curse despite the oracle's advice. On the trip there, an apparition blocked the road he was on. His donkey saw the apparition and stopped. Balaam did not see it. The apparition was holding a sword and was blocking the path. The donkey swerved off the path. Balaam beat the donkey to move ahead. Once more the apparition appeared and again Balaam angrily beat the donkey when she refused to go. The donkey turned to Balaam and asked "What have I done to you to earn such a beating? Have I not served you faithfully?" At this point Balaam saw the apparition and realized that the donkey had saved his life.

It was anger that propelled Balaam to attack his donkey. Anger, like any other emotion, is never meant to be made the provocation for action or words. Angry words and angry actions are destructive, never constructive. Anger blinded

Balaam. The fact that Balaam saw the donkey as his inferior prevented him from examining the donkey's actions and recognizing, given their history together, that the donkey would act only in Balaam's best interest.

• Aphrodite (Venus), while married to Hephaestus, was having an affair with a youth named Ares (Mars). To maintain their privacy, Ares stationed Alectryon at the door to watch for the approach of the Sun. Alectryon fell asleep and Apollo (Sun) came while the lovers were *in flagrante delicto*. They were caught by Venus' husband in each other's arms and were embarrassed before all the gods. Ares was so angered that he changed Alectryon into a rooster who is required to announce the approach of the Sun each day.

• A Chinese proverb says that if I am patient in one moment of emotion, I will escape one hundred days of sorrow.

Word Card 92

ANXIETY

Anxiety has to do with trouble in mind and the uncertainty of a coming event. It flows from a strained desire, something greatly wanted. This often becomes pathological, producing agitation, depression, and sometimes even chest pains. In his movies, Woody Allen expresses angst: Nothing is ever going to turn out right. However, there is really no need to feel distressed or worried. Most foreboding is over concerns that never materialize. The fear and dread which I manifest will only heighten the nervousness I am feeling at the moment. Angst is okay in the movies: I can laugh at it. In real life it can only block my peace of mind.

• Freud taught that neurotic anxiety is nothing more or less than a converted sexual desire.

• Anxiety has always been regarded as a state of possession. To the casual observer it seems as if the ego has been taken over by an alien force.

• Nightmares are clear signals of anxiety, often followed by physical ailments brought on by the anxiety such as a feeling of choking, an inability to swallow, or sometimes even spasms.

• When I encounter a problem which cannot be solved with rational thought or charm, I can choose neurosis. Insanity is often a voluntary state.

• If I become neurotic, the question I should ask myself is how does this serve me? How does the neurosis have value and meaning for me? Having a neurosis forces me into a mode of living which helps me develop my potentialities.

• When I want something badly and fear that which I wish for will not take place, I feel anxiety.

• My secretary's mother and her mother's mother counseled the worrier, "It never happens the way you worry it."

Word Card 93

APOLOGY

This requires an explanation of my actions. Someone affected by my actions needs to know that no harm was intended. Or, when I have offered a poor substitute for what I was to provide (e.g., food; car; room), I offer an apology. Now is the time for me to make a confession. I sit down before an empty chair and image the person with whom I should make amends as sitting in the chair. Out loud I let the person know that there is no excuse for what I have said or done. I make my retraction, I beg the person's pardon, and I bring inner peace to my heart.

Word Card 94

APPEARANCE

Once upon a time there was a goddess, Eos, who was cursed by Aphrodite with a constant longing for young mortals. Secretly and filled with shame, Eos seduced several young men. Finally Eos carried off the sons of Tros, one of whom she lost to Zeus. She begged Zeus to grant the other boy immortality so that they could be lovers forever. Zeus granted her wish, but she forgot to ask also for perpetual youth and her lover grew older each day. He began to wrinkle and his voice grew shrill and when Eos became tired of nursing him he turned into a cicada.

When dealing with appearance, it is very important to remember that everything and everybody are in a constant state of change.

• Appearance means to become visible, present myself to the public, publish my book, or to become conspicuous. It can also refer to standards: Keeping up my appearance or measuring the look of things. Something is emerging in my life, manifesting for the first time. The materialization of whatever it is exposes my hidden desires or unspoken attitudes which have been kept secret until now. I do not let this throw me. I maintain my demeanor and continue to be myself. The word emergency derives from the sense of a sudden coming. I will take care.

Word Card 95

ATTACK

Attack could be an invasion of germs, cancer cells, or a virus. It could be a verbal or physical attack against me or even one launched by me. It could be a game, like chess, where I out-think my opponent and put them on the defense. Or, it could be a difficult project I am about to attack.

Attack expresses a situation of conflict. Symbolically, the struggle may be primordial or cosmogenic, such as the conflict between Osiris, the god of vegetation, and Set, the god of drought. Or, the struggle may be within me, physically or psychologically. Before I start a counterattack, I must remember that it is I that I am attacking. Every expression is self-directed. Whomever I waylay is a symbol of my aggressive feelings toward myself.

• Stentor was one of the Greeks who fought in the Trojan War. The *Iliad* says he had a voice of bronze and that his battle cry was as loud as the cry of fifty other men. In a battle, typically at the point of attack, there is a call to charge from a sergeant with a loud voice or by playing loud notes on a trumpet. The word "stentorian," which means very loud, derives from Stentor's name.

• People with a propensity for violence and aggression against others experience less fear than normal people. Since they have less stress and less fear in confrontations, they engage in antisocial behavior more freely.

Word Card 96

ATTRACTIVE

Attractive is the quality of attracting, which is the force which can draw me in by an invisible influence such as gravity, electromagnetism, or even the pheromones of another. When I experience this, I ask myself whether I am being drawn into this new relationship, business deal, or arrangement out of need or out of greed. Attraction from need is healthy but if it arises out of greed, it would be unattractive given a different scenario. I always remember that in the dark all cats are gray.

• Narcissus was a beautiful lad. He was so attractive that every girl he met wanted to belong to him. He passed up all of them all and would have nothing to do with them. No matter how heartbroken they were, the young maidens got nowhere with Narcissus. Even the fairest of them all, Echo, could not move him. Echo was quite likeable, particularly because of her lively conversation. Hera, a mighty goddess, suspected that Zeus was having an affair with Echo. Her suspicions were unfounded. Nevertheless Hera unjustly placed a curse on Echo and condemned her never to use her tongue again except to repeat what was said to her. This was the greatest punishment of all for Echo.

She was attracted to Narcissus and dearly loved him, but now she could not speak to him. One day she hid in the woods where Narcissus was to pass and when he heard her rustling about he called out "Come." Echo stepped out, held out her arms, and answered joyfully, "Come." Narcissus turned away angrily, "I will die before I give you power over me." Echo humbly repeated the last words she heard, "I give you power over me." A great goddess, Nemesis, heard what had happened. Her name, Nemesis, means Righteous Anger. Her curse on Narcissus was, "May he who loves not others love himself."

As Narcissus passed a pool he saw his image in the water. "Now I know what others have suffered, for I burn with love of my own self. How can I reach that loveliness I see mirrored in the water? I cannot leave it. Only death can set me free." He never looked away from the pool of water. As he was dying, he cried out to his image, "Farewell. Farewell." Echo was nearby and she repeated the words as a final tribute to him. Legend has it that as his spirit crossed the River Styx, it leaned over the boat for a final glimpse of itself. Being attractive to oneself is fatal.

Word Card 97

BEGINNING

That which is entering upon its existence or which is originating has a beginning. It is the initial stage. Anything extended in time or space has a start, such as the beginning of the end. At the starting point of my endeavor, I ask myself how will all this end. I ask myself whether the rocket I am about to launch or the sexual relationship in which I am about to engage will have smooth sailing. I think of myself as the fountainhead. I am the one to whom others look for guidance. I must look beyond the beginning to the end. I remember what the great movie producer Samuel S. Goldwyn said: To start is to finish.

Word Card 98

BOAST

Boasters speak big. I make loud sounds as I brag. More so when I threaten, bully, or terrify. Yet even a humble farmer who speaks only of the treasures of his heart can boast. It is said that she who tooteth not her own horn, the same will not be tooted. It is also said that, *Id me glorior*, this is that in which I glory. Glorying in what I have accomplished is fine until it turns to crowing or swaggering. After all it is more than just the visible me which does anything. It is my invisible self as well. I have to give it some credit as well.

Word Card 99

BOREDOM

I am a true bore when I think that the world is interested in only one subject, the one which I understand. Boredom is a lack of interest in anything except myself and my agenda. When I crave excitement in my life instead of boredom the formula is quite simple. In order to percolate I have to circulate. To get rid of monotony, I will go and play a game of Monopoly® or any game which will break the tedium. Boredom produces tedium and dullness. My dreariness will disappear the moment I become eager and animated about something.

Word Card 100

BOSS

In politics, the boss is the dictator. At work, the boss is the employer. In a relationship, it is the dominant partner. In describing clothes or cars or other possessions as boss, it means the absolute top. It can also refer to a swelling on an animal or a plant. In any event, I am being called upon to control or lord it over others. The kind of leadership I exert will determine the kind of subordinates I will have. If I am overbearing or imperious, I can expect World War III. If I am flexible and pliable, I can expect a symbiotic and caring relationship. When I bring assistance to my assistant, help to my helper, the payoff will be cooperation.

Word Card 101

CHANGE

This means substituting one thing for another or making an alteration in the quality of something. It could be a change of life, a change of the moon, or a change of mates. It means to make things different. All change involves risk because it results in a transformation. Metamorphosis is great for a caterpillar but for the butterfly it means death. When I decide to embark on a change, I cannot be swayed by the novelty of the experience. Rather, I take heart from the joy of the innovation. In other words, I do not engage the change simply for a thrill. I innovate, bringing something new into existence for the benefit of myself or others or for the world to share. The older I get the less likely it is that I will accept change easily. This is all the more reason for me to learn not to resist change when it appears.

• Change is sought by a person who is adaptable and spontaneous. A curious person is also one who is willing to entertain change. Such people need teachers who are flexible and not rigid. Freedom is very important to people who are looking for new avenues and new types of work. People who love change have difficulty making decisions. Routine for them is an invitation to mischief. When the payoff is more freedom, this person is highly motivated.

• Change occurs even before I see it myself. I know very little about my own transformations. People who have not seen me in a long time remark about how I have changed and I have no sense that changes in me have taken place.

Word Card 102

CHILD

When I have reached that agonizing point when an unresolved conflict is tearing me apart, the unconscious psyche always creates a third course, a unifying new birth. It is this which creates a new whole, uniting a pair of opposites. Out of this situation emerges the symbol of the child. It is the symbol which will point to a way and a possibility which the conscious mind could never discover and yet will bring about the needed unification.

• If I am with child, I am pregnant, ready to burst forth with a great new idea. This is a time of innocence. I may be dealing with an immature person or acting in an immature manner myself. The child within me is a description of an important part of me. As the child, I live within my emotional chakra. When I move my feelings into the heart space, I move into adulthood and unconditional love. When I need to be the child, I think of myself as an artist or a storyteller. I draw naif portraits or tell fairy tales and I become the child. It is a wonderful playpen (space) in which to meditate.

• The act of naming a child is much like the Christian ritual of baptism. Both are treated as if they were magical acts. Both create a personality or a soul for the child. When the child is named for a deceased ancestor it is as if the ancestor is being reborn. The soul of the ancestor is revived and implanted in the child.

When I give a name to a child, I am giving it the power of that name. It is for this reason that the names of saints are given to children at baptism. When I create or make up a name for a child, I am creating a new energy for the child.

• When the child motif appears in the reading, it represents something that formerly existed which is something that is happening right now as well. Seen in this light, I see its purpose as compensating for or correcting some exaggeration in my conscious mind.

• Adults like to think of trivial matters as child's play.

Word Card 103

COMIC

I am in a situation which is calculated to make me laugh. Comedy is on the same stick with its opposite, tragedy. I ask myself if I am in the comic pages or the tragic pages of life. Will I be entertained or will I entertain others? Pythagoras never laughed, nor did he cry. He remained balanced. Before I leave home each day I go and stand in front of my mirror and make a face. I do something absurd. I let my inner joker hold sway. Then I go to work and all day whenever anything annoys me, I remember the face of the comic and smile.

• An offbeat sense of humor gives me an air of charm. I am somber most of the time but there is an inner joker within me ready to let loose.

Word Card 104

COMPULSION

Those who do things to me against my will are using compulsion. Compulsion eliminates choice and freedom. When compulsion takes over, it produces strange urges, even addiction. In order to avoid the inescapable consequences of compulsion, I look for additional choices. I seek a more permissive atmosphere.

• The name Jonah means "dove." Dove is a traditional symbol for Israel (*Psalms* 74:19) Jonah is the embodiment of intolerance and bigotry. His strong feelings of ill will towards the Gentiles of Nineveh contrast greatly with the feelings of good will felt by the Good Samaritan in a corresponding parable told by Jesus. Both stories speak of the world's wickedness. Jonah is reluctant to do anything about it and the Samaritan is powerless not to.

• The Good Samaritan is acting under a compulsion.

• Whenever I am constantly looking for that which is novel, I become bored with conditions which are stable. I greet new situations with great intensity. My regular life is left behind. This is compulsion. When my stable home life or workplace feels like a prison, nothing will deter me from disrupting the status quo.

• Compulsion is replete with danger. I can lose everything I have, relationships, job, home, by frittering away my time chasing other ties rather than staying put. When I abandon my own fields which need tending in order to share in another harvest, I am sure to wind up with an empty barn.

Word Card 105

CONFORM

Organized religion sometimes impinges upon individual expression of imagination. A good example is the Second Commandment which prohibits the making of images. (*Exodus* 20:2) The priests of Baal, a widespread religion, were murdered by Jehu (*II Kings* 10:50) because they worshiped idols. Later when Israel's army set out to do battle with Canaan, God reminded them to destroy all of Canaan's art work and sculpture. (*Numbers* 33:52) Being required to conform curbs the imagination. Nonetheless, there are times when conformity is appropriate because to conform is to act in harmony and accord not only with others but also with myself, both of which are desirable.

• To conform means leading a life that is structured, orderly, and planned. Taking all things into careful consideration leads to successful execution. There will be time to do other things.

Word Card 106

CONFUSION

When I am lost, I find the way when I remember that the maze begins and ends with me, not with another. It is up to me to discover the path because each person's path is different. Sometimes confusion results from distraction or from my failure to pay close attention.

• A Hans Christian Andersen fairy tale tells the story of a hungry dog who lives in a valley between two mountains. On top of each mountain sits a castle. When it is time for the dog to eat, a trumpet is sounded. One day the dog hears a trumpet and starts running up the mountain.

Half way up, the trumpet stops and the dog hears the trumpet call from the second mountain. He runs back to the bottom thinking that the food would be gone from the first mountaintop and starts up the second mountain. Just then the second trumpet stopped blowing. This goes on for awhile until both trumpets are silent and all the food is gone.

• Confusion always makes me do things which result in no gain. Until confusion abates I run myself ragged and go nowhere.

• The unconscious has both backward and forward potential. In the backward direction are the ancient instincts and in the forward direction are the fates. None of this is cognizable by my conscious mind, nor is it a part of the conscious ego. When the unconscious takes over the role of the ego, confusion is the inevitable result. A person who works at making the unconscious dominant is courting insanity. Excesses in love or hatred or in joy or grief are enough to allow my ego to change places with my unconscious. When I find myself saying or doing things which are far out of the ordinary, I am in a state of confusion.

Word Card 107

CYCLE

I am moving in circles, chasing my own tail. The round of events has yet to run its course. This card can also mean that there is (or will be) a course of medical treatment which will be necessary. Cycles are always divided into times of action and inaction. If the activity does not include a period of inactivity, it is not a cycle. A cycle is also always rhythmical. The stop and go of the cycle becomes musical. Finally, a cycle has a Zeitgeist, a spirit that describes it. The Zeitgeist of the Thirties was the Depression. The Twenties was the era of the flapper while the Sixties was the period when sex came out of the closet. I look at the cycle I am in and define its Zeitgeist.

• This card is a reminder of the creation process, the coming together of the pairs of extremes. Each has a cycle and each appears in due course. Light did not appear in our cosmos until a billion years after the Big Bang. Yet it was always there. Night cannot exist without day. Illness cannot exist without well-being. The union and balance of well-being and illness equal the harmony of health. There is no such thing as good health or bad health, only the cycle of health.

• Everything in the Cosmos vacillates from one extreme to the other: Active and passive, masculine and feminine, birth and death. The two principles represented in all extremes balance each other. The cycle is the essence of the power of creation, an ebb and a flow, first one thing and then the other. Everything stems from its inner polarity.

• Early life is represented by steady forward movement featuring constant increase. Later life features a steady decrease. An attempt to live the second half as if it were the first half disrupts the cycles. Both parts of life have a purpose with attendant meaning.

Word Card 108

DANGER

There is an expression, out of debt, out of danger. When I owe nothing (not just money or material things) I escape the karmic consequences. The original meaning of danger is the power that someone has to hurt me. When I pay that someone what it is I owe, danger disappears. A sense of insecurity can create a feeling of danger within me. I look out for a booby trap but the booby trap is a phantom creation of my own foreboding. I become very vulnerable when I live with a sense of danger.

Word Card 109

DEPEND

To depend means to be held in a form of suspense. I rely on another who holds the rope on which I am suspended. Supply is spiritual; money is congealed energy. There is no need to depend on another whose breath is in his nostrils. Rather I take the position that I am the person on whom others can rely. Self-sufficiency is a spiritual principle. Its benefits are independence and autonomy. Notice that depend is negated in independence.

• In *Tao Te Ching*, Lao-tzu wrote that there is something formless yet complete that existed before heaven and earth which was without sound or substance, was dependent on nothing, and was unchanging. One may think of it as the mother of all things under heaven. Because we do not know its true name, "Way" is the name that we give it.

• To achieve a state where I depend on nothing and no person, I must be without prejudice in order to have room for everyone and everything. I must bring about a union of the opposites within me, becoming a symbol both of what is and what is not.

• This card alerts me to the possibility that I can move to a state of self-dependence.

Word Card 110

DESTROY

In Greek mythology, there is the story of Cassandra, who became a prophetess. Apollo had been in love with her and had bestowed upon her the power to foretell the future. Once she had the gift, Cassandra rejected Apollo's overtures. She knew that divine favors, once bestowed, cannot be taken back. Apollo was furious. No matter what, she would always be able to prophesy. He finally hit upon the perfect revenge: Henceforth no one would believe Cassandra and thereafter no one did. Cassandra tried to tell the populace that Greeks were hidden in the wooden horse at Troy but no one would believe her. It became her fate to always know about approaching disaster and be unable to prevent it.

When Apollo set out to destroy Cassandra, he wanted to get even. Since he could not take back the gift, he made it of no account. He nullified it. To destroy means to take away what a person has and all that she will ever have.

This means undoing that which has been built, putting it out of existence. It is a killing of sorts, a demolition. When I quench a fire, I destroy it. When I erase what I have written or undo a relationship, I have also destroyed. When destruction is hurtful, it is at the other end of the stick with creation. It is much easier to destroy than to create. For this reason, I meditate and think before I undo. When I destroy, it is as if I have eliminated a species. There can be no recovery or restoration.

• Inner destruction makes me feel like the world is coming to an end. Chaos reigns. An investment has gone sour. A spouse has deserted me. A loved one has passed. An injury has left me disabled. Any of a multitude of incidents has the potential of bringing me to a state of disorientation. It is at this instant, at the point of collapse, that the unconscious takes over. Perhaps I hear a "still small voice" with the answer to my problem or perhaps a vision or hallucination gives me an idea I can use to save the day.

Word Card 111

DISGRACE

Dis is a slang word meaning to show disrespect or affront, belittle, insult, or disparage. If I disgrace a person or a cause I, too, am a disgrace. The question is who has gained by this. A person in disgrace is out of favor. Being out of favor can be shameful for me or bring ignominy. Alternatively, it can be seen as a natural adjustment in my life.

Word Card 112

DISLIKE

Dislike is the extreme of like. When loathing becomes my way of life, cynicism is not far behind. Cynicism is a defense born from my sense of being incapable of competing with others. Therefore, I dislike them. When nothing suits my fancy, I am reminded that I am the common denominator in all the dissatisfaction. To enjoy is to delight in life. To dislike it is to shun life.

• Dislike is an emotion which easily rises to hatred. When I accumulate many dislikes, I can convert them into hatreds without too much effort.

• A person who is troubled by an inferiority complex will always have a compensating need to dislike or hate others. To dislike is an activity which has its roots in the person who does the disliking. If I dislike another, I ask myself what it is about me which is resonating to something in the other person. When I dislike another, I am giving that person undue importance. No one is so important to me that I have to dislike him or her.

Word Card 113

DREAM

All symbols owe their creation to the ability of the human being to dream. Dreams occupy a large percentage of my life since I spend about a third of each day asleep and a large part of that time dreaming. I treat this picture card as a dream and interpret it. A dream is a series of emotional images which passes through my mind while I am asleep and is a message to the conscious. Dreams are my own personalized mythology.

• My mind has certain inherited tendencies to form particular images. These images are representative of me and the events which form my experiences. These tendencies do not originate in my conscious mind, rather in my unconscious. Once I can identify these tendencies and learn to understand what they represent, I can achieve harmony and balance.

• Some things are so beautiful or so stupendous that they can only be seen in a dream.

Word Card 114

ELIMINATE

This means to thrust out of doors, getting something out of the place in which I live because it has no function and no relevance. It is the same as a good bowel movement. I give little thought to that which I eliminate. I have gotten rid of it. Yet it has life or it fits into my scheme and here I am about to eliminate it. I must give thought to whether this is a good decision. I may be throwing the baby out with the bathwater.

Word Card 115

EMBARRASS

To have an embarrassment of riches means to have more money than I know what to do with. On the other hand if I cannot pay my dinner bill I will be embarrassed. To embarrass means to put another in difficulty. It means to create an obstacle. To remember a long-ago event with embarrassment means that I have uncovered an area of concern – a hot spot – which has been brought to my consciousness. Whatever shames me or upsets me describes an important aspect of my patterning.

• Whenever I feel embarrassed, I am unable to focus attention on matters at hand. In such a state I am concerned only with that which is the source of my embarrassment. To mortify is to edify.

Word Card 116

EROTIC

The *Song of Solomon* provides an example of erotic expression. It is a mystical magnetism. On a personal level, erotic refers to an inner integration and unification. Eroticism can be distinguished from pornography by virtue of its mystic symbolism. Sexual intercourse is a coming together of opposites. It is a sign of harmony.

• A strong erotic wish which is unfulfilled will generate a dream of anxiety. If I repress that which is erotic during the day, eroticism will be the subject-matter of my dreams.

Word Card 117

EXPERT

Experience equates to knowledge. It can be gained through participation or through observation. This means that I learn every moment because every moment is an experience. To become a connoisseur or a professional or a virtuoso means that I have undergone training and practice: Experience makes me an expert. The first step to expertise is to be a willing novice anxious to become a master. An expert deals in facts and details, is focused on the here and now, and brings creativity to bear.

Word Card 118

FAIL

When I fail, I am wanting; my word means nothing. When I give way to an enemy, I lose my power. Crops may fail, my heart may wane, my eyes may dim. To fail may mean that I am about to become insolvent. My aim is to carry out my project to full term. To stop in the middle or before I finish is to fail.

When I say that I will do something without fail, it means that I am strengthening my promise. I must change fail into without fail.

Word Card 119

FASCINATION

Serpents by their look and sometimes by their perceived presence deprive their prey of the power of resistance. Famous people have this same power over crowds. Individuals do it to each other. Fascination is the casting of a spell. The attraction is irresistible; judgment becomes impaired and faculties are enslaved. When I sense that I have become transfixed, it is my chance to return to normalcy. To become so absorbed that I become a captive of a relationship or situation is living as one who is hypnotized.

Life becomes more fascinating when I develop my intuitive skills. Fascination means that I have dropped that which is routine and gone on to explore patterns and relationships. When I am fascinated by something or somebody, I look for inner meanings. It means that I become better with learning new skills rather than using old ones. I like to work with questions and problems which have more than one answer.

Word Card 120

FATHER

My nearest male relative is my father. The person to whom I owe my religious life is my father. The person who acts like a father to me may be an older friend, teacher, relative, minister, or rabbi, some person who is not my biological father. If I have reached the stage in my life in which I adopt the role of father for others, I must accept the responsibility which goes with the role. Being father means being more than acting as a sperm donor. Being father is an ordination. I am acting as priest for the benefit of others.

• In fairy tales and myths, the father of the hero is often a woodsman or a master craftsman. An Arabian legend tells us that Terah, the father of Abraham was an artisan who could sculpt and who could cut a shaft from a piece of wood. The Jewish legend about Terah makes him a crafter of images of the deity. In Arabic usage, a man who can cut a shaft is a begetter of great sons. Joseph, the father of Jesus, was a carpenter. Cinyras, the father of Adonis, was also a carpenter. Cinyras is credited with inventing the hammer and the lever. The father of Hermes was Hephaestus, a sculptor.

• The father in the unconscious is a personification of spirit as a procreator. This is the reason why father in myths and fairy tales is a man who can make things in a masterful way. The father is the one who crafts the hero so to speak and brings him into existence. The father propels the hero.

• The hero symbolizes the unconscious self. It is the embodiment of all the archetypes, including the father archetype. Thus the hero is his own begetter.

• An abnormal dependence on either parent by a child remains latent in the personality well into adulthood. In spite of having maintained a job or profession and a marriage for years, there often appears an irrational blockage or even a breakdown when such a condition is carried over from childhood. Suddenly everything which goes wrong is because the father or the mother is standing in the way. This suggests that it is an unconscious aspect of the person's own personality which is bringing forth the father's image and not a situation which is external. Liberation from the past is possible once there is an understanding that the source of the difficulty emanates from within.

• The father strives to be the supreme moral authority, sort of a "Father Knows Best." This authority figure carefully examines what everyone's conscience should be doing, deciding what is right and what is wrong. Father is an inhibiting symbol, someone who has castrated me. My attempts at independence are being thwarted. The father, who is judgmental by nature, has a collection of sayings which he uses according to the situation. This father is opinionated and sees himself as God's representative.

• The Catholic Church calls its priests "Father" in order to mark them as superior wise men, capable of leading a flock as if it were a family.

FEAR

Alfred Hitchcock understood the concept of instilling a sense of fear in his audiences. He would let you know where the danger was. Then you would watch as the unsuspecting victim approached it. When I feel fear it is as if I can picture danger as just around the corner. It is the same in the dream world or in the conscious world as it is in the Hitchcock films. I create the unseen danger in my imagination in order to bring on the fright. Fear is dispelled when I dissolve the ghosts.

Fear is the emotion of the pain caused by impending danger. The state of alarm I sense is that something or someone I do not care for is about to become a source of real danger. When I have mixed feelings of dread and reverence, my fear is of a deity or other rightful authority. The apprehension I sense or the trepidation I feel as I approach the unknown can be nothing more than an unexplainable nightmare.

• When I fantasize a disastrous occurrence, such as my house burning down, and I see my loved ones at risk and do nothing about it, I am describing my own depressive ideas and convictions. Inner fantasies and disasters in which I do not play a helping role describe how I feel about myself. I have so many negative suggestions about myself that they manifest in these fantasies of fear. Since there is no intellectual or rational basis for my fears, I understand that these fantasies are coming from my unconscious. The solution is to participate actively in the fantasy: Run in and save the people from the fire or leap into the ocean and save the drowning person. In this way I recapture the expenditure of energy by the unconscious and return it to the conscious. The unconscious begins to lose its dominance and, almost like magic, the negative suggestions begin to diminish. What I have done is simply to change my conscious attitude.

• People who are highly emotional often have great fear of reality because the individual self and the persona are both mired in the unconscious. For them the world we see and live in becomes the unconscious content. Emotional people with an artistic bent are very susceptible to this aberration.

• Fear is also expressed in the dream world. It often comes when I am about to embark on a new project or engage a wholly new set of relationships or even get married. Often it is the inner child expressing a typical uncertainty in a new situation. The word I use to describe that which upsets me tells where I am in experiencing the fear. If I use the word scary, I am in the child motif. If I use the word fright, I am in the adult motif.

Word Card 122

FIRM

Firm may be the name of a business. It can refer to that which never wavers and which is securely fixed. I may have in mind an offer I have made or received; it is firm. A person is firm who is said to be steadfast. The boat that is anchored cannot sail. It remains stationary. On the other hand some situations require me to remain constant and not to waver. It is better for me to be firm than to fluctuate.

• That which is firm is rooted. It goes deep and its growth is from below upward and from above downward. When I am seen as firm, it means that I can be depended upon to be the same tomorrow as I was yesterday and as I am today.

• A tree is the symbol of that which is solid, permanent, and firmly rooted. If the tree cannot sway with the wind, the trunk or limbs may break.

Word Card 123

GAME

I could be playing games or playing a good game or my game may be up. What I must remember is that all games have rules and also that breaking these rules brings on repercussions. If I am game for life, my spirit is balanced. I will be neither the chaser nor the chased. The card's basic meaning is as a symbol of a struggle. I am struggling against my fears and weaknesses. Even when I play a game for fun, I still want to win and bask in the victory. The reason is that the outer game mimics the ongoing inner game which this card brings to mind. Life itself is a game, one which has predetermined roadways. One of these roadways is uniquely mine. It is my patterning. Once I learn it, I step in and live it.

• A game can have either of two endings: Happy or sad. There are games which end with me laughing and others which disappoint me and leave me crying.

Word Card 124

GIVE

The only thing I have to give is myself. When I eat a good meal I am eating the cook. The guests at my table are the recipients of myself. When I donate to the poor or the homeless, I do it anonymously. I distribute gifts at holidays without any expectation of reciprocation. Giving is not a quid pro quo process. I feel that I am blessed. This means that my prosperity has been bestowed on me so that I can disburse it to others. To be blessed does not mean that I can horde the monies I earn or receive. I become the custodian for giving. Indeed I should live well. The requirement for achieving wholeness is that I should also give well.

Word Card 125

GO

To remain steady as she goes is to keep my ship of life in balance. I intend to make a go of the project or relationship I am involved with. It will succeed. My motto is go for it! This card also speaks of an approaching passing away, a retirement from one phase of life to another, a leave-taking, a departure. When I am working well I have "get up and go." I have stamina and pep. When I go, I make progress. When I stop, I am at rest.

Word Card 126

GRIEF

What begins as grief sometimes turns into self-pity. The first set of my tears is legitimate. Anything after that becomes me feeling sorry for myself. Whatever the loss, whatever I have done, whatever the disaster, it is over. Remorse will not undo it. I make my grief short-lived. Turning grief into joy seems impossible. Yet for every Good Friday there is an Easter Sunday. For every labor pain, a child is born. I think of how that which troubles me is serving me and my grief disappears.

• In the *Iliad* is a description of a vineyard filled with young people singing "a sweet Linus song." Linus was the son of Apollo and Psamathe. His mother deserted him and he was brought up by shepherds. He was a gentle and sweet youth who, before he was fully grown, was torn to pieces by dogs. The Greeks coined a phrase *ailinon* which literally means woe for Linus. To this day it is used to express grief. In English the word *alas* means the same thing: How could this tragedy have happened!

Word Card 127

GUILT

My conscience is bothering me. I am condemning myself after doing something I never would do ordinarily. If my sense of culpability persists, it means that not only am I the judge who has convicted me, I am also the executioner. Guilt is the one feeling which cannot be relieved.

• Guilt arises when two aspects within me have formed a conflicting whole. For example, if I as a married person behave as if I am single and form other intimate relationships, I will become afflicted by a sense of guilt. The dark shadow emerges as morals are subverted. When my behavior becomes disconcerting to others the conflict becomes dangerous.

Word Card 128

HABIT

Habit is that which is second nature to me. It is the way I am mentally constituted. It is my patterning, my settled tendencies. Or, it could be the clothes which I wear and which have a sameness to them. Style is something about me which I can create. I look in the mirror. This is my style, the habitual way I have of presenting myself to the world. My customary manner of behaving should be examined. Some of my habits serve me well. Some will be discarded. Compulsive habits which become addictions may be counterproductive.

• My positive habits strengthen me. If I keep a garden I form a relationship with my plants and flowers. If I regularly attend my place of worship I benefit from spiritual nourishment and at the same time develop my ability to socialize with others. Not going to my house of worship regularly is just as great a habit as going. Whatever I repeat frequently eventually becomes involuntary.

• Habits are adventitious. Any habit can attach to any individual. I may become tight with money no matter my station in life. In other words I am not programmed to pick up any particular habit or to disdain others. Habits are an anomaly. They are acquired through free will but once acquired cannot be discarded through free will.

• The word *education* derives from Latin words which mean to lead out or to draw out of oneself. This is the process by which a habit is broken. A habit is patterned behavior which has overcome my will. It is my will which becomes the subject of the educative process.

• When I break one habit, I have broken a thousand habits. Habits are like dominoes. Any habit can start the fall of all the others when it is broken.

Word Card 129

HATE

Hate is the extreme end of love. The venom which a snake carries in its pouch is symbolic of hate. The venom is thrust out through the tube-like teeth at lightning speed into the snake's enemy or prey. This is why hate is called venom. When I carry hate within my heart venom has made a home there, ready to shoot out at the handiest target.

• Hate is an active feeling. If I am a bearer of hate, I am always on the lookout for a target of my hatred. When I live in hatred I live in strife. Hatred and revenge are twins. Families who hold feuds become famous for their hatreds. Hate is always present where vice is practiced.

• Hate is reserved for certain situations. I hate not keeping a promise. I know someone who hates being late. Most people hate ingratitude.

• Hate is the best barometer for describing the real me. The more I hate the more I am describing myself.

Word Card 130

HESITATION

Doubt about which course of action would be more likely to succeed is hesitation. I have a stammering of the mind. To vacillate because of scruples means that I am not fully developed in my own sense of morality. To hesitate because of qualms means that I am dealing with pollution and contamination. To hesitate because of self-doubt means that I have no confidence in my own ability. To remain indecisive means that I lack information. I examine the reason for my hesitation.

• When I am caught up in a confused state because I am lost, there is an inevitable hesitation. Each way I turn there is a blockage. Symbolically, I am caught in a labyrinth. The labyrinth is a primordial image which I encounter in mythology, fantasy, and dreams.

• The inextricable maze built by Daedalus is featured prominently in Grecian mythology. If I am driving on a road which is not familiar to me and suddenly realize I am passing a spot I passed earlier, I have the sense of being in a labyrinth. Or, I may find myself in a dream in which I descend to the underworld where I encounter one false trail after another. Finally, a snake coiled up replicates the design a labyrinth.

• Necessity demands that I make an important decision. Yet I hesitate. Too many interests are pulling me in diverse directions. When I find myself spiritually, mundane matters sort themselves out.

Word Card 131

HIDE

A hide is the skin of an animal, something I use for clothing, shoes, or a purse. My hide or my exterior makes the inner me invisible and knowable only by me. Therefore it also means putting myself out of sight, hiding my face like an ostrich. One of my favorite childhood games was hide and seek. Before I left to go seek those who had hidden I yelled, "All hid?" Now I am hiding. I listen for the call. When I camouflage my inner self, I defraud two people: Myself and another. Everyone wears a mask of one sort or another. To the extent that my outer mask matches who I really am is a determinant of my proximity to wholeness.

• When I can find neither hide nor hair of that which I seek, someone or something is lost.

• I hide my face when I feel shame or embarrassment.

• Hiding my face in sand means that I refuse to face up to a troublesome problem.

• If I am afflicted with a sense of modesty, I may become prone to hiding my light under a bushel instead of lighting a candle. (*Matthew* 5:15)

Word Card 132

HOLDING ON

In Hebrew, the verb "to sin" means "to miss the mark." To maintain my aim I have to hold on. I have to carry on, to maintain my course of action or movement. The French have an expression, *tenez bon, on arrive.* It means that I should hold on because help is on the way. When persevering in doing what I know is morally correct, I can withstand all assaults, verbal and otherwise. The true martyr never loses heart, never despairs and digs in for a lasting struggle. The false martyr sacrifices self for undeserving others. The true martyr has a cause, the false martyr has none. I make sure I always have something onto which I can hold.

• When I was a child, I needed an adult to hold me on my bicycle. When I find myself in an emotional hotspot, I reach inside for my inner adult. My inner child is of no value to me at these moments.

• When I am about to do something and someone asks me to hold on, I am being asked to wait or stop. Sometimes I am warned from within to hold on, not to move precipitously.

Word Card 133

HOME

Home is a place of nurturing, the place where I live. Therefore when I am homeless, I am destitute, I have no refuge. At home, I have no constraints. Situations outside my physical home can give me that same good feeling. Some feel at home on horseback; others are at home in an amusement park. This at home feeling is so powerful that when visitors come we put them at ease and make them feel at home. At home I am free from attack: I cannot get picked off at home plate. I am always trying to reach home or call home. Going to the heart of a matter is going home, my place of final rest. Once upon a time I was in a cradle. Someone took care of me, caressed me, and loved me. I was sheltered, fed, and made to feel comfortable. Whenever I am tempted to attack or disrespect those who cared for me, I call forth the days I cannot remember, the days when my place of origin was my first home. I will never know who held me as an infant besides my family. I like to imagine that a person of great and powerful love held me.

• The ever-recurrent theme about home in fairy tales, myths, legends, and religious text is that someone is always leaving home. Sometimes the leaving is involuntary as in the expulsion from the Garden of Eden. Sometimes it is because of a quest such as with Abraham's. In the case of Cain, it was because he had committed a heinous crime. Hagar was put out of her home because of her dispute with Sarah. The prodigal son returned home out of desperation. These stories illustrate the high value placed on the concept of "home." For in the end, the reader comes away with the thought that returning home is the grandest prize.

Word Card 134

HOMOSEXUAL

There is a period in the life of every human being when an attraction is felt for persons of the same sex. It is a stage in psychosexual development occurring during prepuberty in the male and during early adolescence in the female during which libidinal gratification is sought with members of the same sex. This card asks me to harken back to that period in my life for the answer to my question. It does not mean that I am gay although it could mean that my sexual urges are so suppressed that I make no admissions, not even to myself.

Word Card 135

HOPE

The three heavenly graces are faith, hope, and charity. It is hope which has given me the feeling of trust and confidence which I now have. I expect something which I desire. I expect a promise to be kept. To despair is to be out of hope. When I allow doubt into the equation I am giving up hope. It is said that over the gates to the entrance of Hell is the inscription, "Abandon hope, all ye who enter here." To adopt pessimism as my standard or to live with fear would be to abandon hope.

• When I say I will cross my heart and hope to die, I am telling the whole truth.

Word Card 136

HUMILIATE

Humility is an excellent tool for rejuvenation especially if done in private such as with a lover. When it is done in public it is a mortification. To behave deferentially is a role I have to play at some time or other. To appear meek or modest, even self-effacing does not necessarily mean that I am the one who has been humiliated. The most insignificant person or child I know has some very significant things to say. I honor the lowly. I exalt the unpretentious.

• Lucretia was the wife of Tarquinius, a king of Rome. She was cruelly raped by a nobleman. She told her husband what had happened. She felt so humiliated that she stabbed herself with a dagger. Shakespeare wrote a play about this called *The Rape of Lucrece.* To humiliate another means to deprive that person of dignity.

Word Card 137

JOY

Joy is an emotion of pure pleasure and supreme well-being. Ecstasy is a momentary sensation which lasts forever. I will never forget a moment of ecstasy and all during my life I recall it to experience more joy. Learning gaiety is an art. If I go around filled with worry, I do not find delight in everyday pleasures. The night should not fall before I have a treat in order to engender joy. Joy is a very necessary ingredient in my life and easy to find in a smile or a dish of chocolate ice cream.

Word Card 138

INTIMIDATE

The key to the word *intimidate* is the *timid* within it. I am using force or force is being used upon me to deter some action. Force and violence inspire artificial fear. Part of the fright I feel stems from the timidity within me which compels me to cower at the first sign of a bully. When I am being browbeaten in a relationship, the choices are fight, flight, or soft answers.

Word Card 139

LAUGHTER

Humankind is the only species which laughs. Laughter is that rare combination of bodily phenomena (facial distortion, inarticulate sounds, shaking of my sides, even tears) which signals an instinctive expression of mirth. Consider that Pythagoras neither laughed nor did he cry. My mother used to say laugh before breakfast; cry before supper. I bring laughter and tears together in balance. There is laughter and there is laughter. Laughter which mocks or belittles another is primarily taunting. It is not real laughter. It is a process of ridiculing in which the snickering is masquerading as laughter. Real laughter is involuntary and contagious. It builds into a crescendo like a flood tide, starting with a smile and a giggle and ends up with roaring laughter.

• In the story of Jonah, God has given him what Jonah regards as an impossible task. He, a devout Jew, is ordered to take God's word to Nineveh, a hotbed of Gentiles. Jonah resents the order because of his bigotry: He detests the Gentiles. He fears that they might accept his message, repent, and be pardoned by God. After his experience with the whale he goes to Nineveh and the Gentiles do accept his message. Even then Jonah continues to sulk, wondering if God will now spare the Ninevites from destruction. In a rare display of divine humor, God asks Jonah whether he should not spare Nineveh from his wrath given the fact that there were so many guiltless infants and harmless cattle. (*Jonah* 3:3-4:11)

• If I profit financially and people deride me, I can laugh all the way to the bank.

Word Card 140

LETTING GO

Letting go means that I am allowing something to escape. I am dismissing someone or somebody from my thoughts. It is time to give vent to my own enthusiasm. I dismiss all negatives. I have been tolerating a lot of nonsense, making concessions which I should not make. All this I must let go. I will learn not to allow things or persons entering my life to poison it. There is no need for me to be abused. My addiction, whether to a substance or to a person, can be released and let go. I can let go by letting off some steam. Or, I can let go by letting someone off the hook.

• The French painter and sculptor, Henri Matisse, was trained as a lawyer. He was working in a law office when he was stricken with appendicitis. During his recuperation he turned to painting. He returned to law but soon realized that his life's passion was to master color. Matisse made the crucial decision of letting go of his original profession and moving into the place where he could follow his bliss.

Word Card 141

LIE

A white lie is a conscious falsehood which becomes praiseworthy because it saves someone's feelings. However, most lies are grossly deceptive and are on the first prong of the ladder. The second prong is theft, and the third prong is a physical attack upon someone. On the other hand the card also means having sex with another, or having my ship lie at anchor, or simply lying prostrate like an animal. If I am tempted to tell a deceitful story which ridicules or brings harm to another, it is the same as if I were to commit an unprovoked attack upon another. My effort is to always speak as if my words will live forever.

• There are big lies and little lies, white lies and black lies. For liars, there is no truth in anything they say. When I lie low, I have to wait until the trouble blows over.

Word Card 142

MEN

A group of men cannot be addressed as such if

there are no women around. Men can only exist as men when women are part of the event. Men by themselves are only half the equation. That which I am doing is missing a very necessary component. Men become assaultive when their only role models are other men who are assaultive.

• Western culture celebrates male dominance and female submission. For me this has become the definition of an erotic heterosexual relationship. Men look for strategies to exert proprietary control over women. This card invites me to examine my potential for violence before it occurs.

Word Card 143

MOTHER

My first learning is from a mother or mother-surrogate. Mother tongue, mother country, mother church are all references to my permanent roots. I am dealing with some fundamental aspect of myself which needs mothering or protection from change. At birth I emerge from my mother's womb. At death I return to the Earth. Prisoners in jails, soldiers on the battlefield, and patients coming out of anaesthesia after surgery all cry out for their mothers. Their call is a yearning to touch the fountainhead and to relive the mothering and nurturing they once received.

• An abnormal dependence on either parent by a child remains latent in the personality well into adulthood. In spite of having maintained a job or profession and a marriage for years, there often appears an irrational blockage or even a breakdown when such a condition is carried over from childhood and a parental image, mother or father, stands in the way. Liberation from the past is possible once there is an understanding that the source of the difficulty is within the person, that it is not outside of the person.

Word Card 144

NAKED

A naked accusation is one made which is unsupported by proof. Something that is visible to the naked eye is the truth without embellishment. This card means there is no concealment. Disguise has been stripped away. After Adam touched the Tree of Good and Evil, he covered his genitals with a fig leaf. God asks him who told him that he was naked. To be undressed means that I cannot lie and, if I cannot lie, it means that all the evil I have done will be exposed. The card alerts me to the possibility that something about me which is private is about to become public.

Word Card 145

OWE

When I bear good will or ill will towards another I am inclined to say, "I owe you one." To owe is to be under an obligation to perform in one way or another. When a debt is outstanding it occupies part of my consciousness. For this reason, Shakespeare has Polonius say that one should neither borrow nor lend. The debt becomes part of the character of both parties. Rather than borrow, I should beg. Rather than lend, I should give.

Word Card 146

PAIN

Pain is the opposite (or the extreme) of pleasure. When I take pains to do something or when it pains me to disclose some fact or detail, it is an exertion signifying either physical or psychic distress. Pain can be either. An ache in my little toe can command more attention of my consciousness than a Wagnerian opera. The slightest discomfort is an unconscious reminder of the transitory nature of man.

- When someone is a pain, they can give you a headache.

Word Card 147

POSTURE

My posture is how I am thinking and feeling at the moment, what role I am assuming for the time being. I pose and therefore posture according to my role – parent, child, teacher, friend, stranger, lawyer, doctor, and so on. My physical body assumes that posture appropriate to my mental or spiritual thinking. I can also posture affairs or relationships in much the same way. Everything about me gives away the entire story. If I am a good enough actor, I can change my attitude, my stance, my bearing, even my demeanor in order to create a false posture. I am not a good enough actor to carry it off. My posture gives me away.

Word Card 148

POWER-PLAY

Fishing demonstrates the notion of power-play. Imagine that I am holding a fishing pole. I give play to the fish until it is the right moment to exercise my power and yank the fish from the water. I am wielding power, affecting things strongly. Whether my power is exercised as fair play or foul play is up to me. A power-play is knowing how to play my cards right.

Word Card 149

RESENT

To resend means to send back again. *Resent* is the past tense of *resend* and means that I have already sent something back. Now I have regret. First I was injured as a result of something someone has done to me or to a loved one. I felt indignant. Now I have a strong feeling of ill will. I must decide when this cycle ends. Good will trumps ill will. Understanding triumphs over antagonism. Resentment promotes rancor and acrimony. When I learn to drop resentment, the cycle will end.

• The fairy tale, "Beauty and the Beast," is named for its two main characters. Beauty is really Little Beauty whose two older sisters are extremely jealous of her, not just because of her beauty but also because of her easy temperament. The tale ends when the Beast is transformed into a handsome prince because of Little Beauty's ability to love the Beast. The jealous sisters who had conspired to bring harm to Little Beauty were transformed into two statues. Their biggest punishment was in witnessing their sister's happiness. To resent another is to be envious of that person. To recover from an envious temperament is a miracle.

Word Card 150

RESIST

When I am dyeing cloth, I apply a substance to the areas not to be colored and it resists the dye. To resist means to withstand the effect of some force. So I learn to resist temptation, resist being influenced, or even to resist disease. Florence Shinn taught what she called the law of nonresistance. It means simply that I allow what is happening to happen without trying to counter it. I will fuel it with none of my energy.

Word Card 151

RETREAT

In the military, retreat is the signal to retire from the field. In a religious setting, it is a withdrawal to meditation and seclusion. In everyday life, a retreat puts me into a place of safety. It is my inner hiding place. Unless inaction plays as important a role as action in my life, I am on a merry-go-round which has no destination. I can get off the wheel if I can learn to retreat. Retreat is self-preservation.

Word Card 152

RIGID

To be rigid is to be fixed in my opinions or unyielding in my ritual observances. Things must be exact and precise. When I am rigid, I am tense. My mind is taut. Being ramrod straight is fine for a Marine. Easygoing is better for everyday living. I never see a rigid bum or a rigid prostitute. They are pliable and relaxed. If I remain rigid, I repel others.

Word Card 153

RIVAL

The word *rival* has its origins in the word *rivus,* meaning stream, which was borrowed directly from the word *rivalis*, a rival in love or – its first meaning – a person who shares the same stream. A rival is one who lives on an opposite shore. I am in competition and trying to outdo the another person who is my mirror-image. All of my competitors behave exactly as I do. We imitate each other and both of us are striving for the same prize. I must slow the pace. I must call off the contest. I will cross the creek before it rises.

Word Card 154

ROT

Rot describes natural decomposition of the physical state. This card may also indicate unsuspected moral or social decay. Rot spreads and will lead to disintegration unless it is cut out at its place of origin. It is apparent when something is going bad in a relationship: Rot is eating away at the relationship when the bright sunny dispositions disappear, holidays are overlooked, good manners lapse. Everything which dies rots, sometimes the rot begins while there is still life.

• When an idea rots, it stinks. Rot is nonsense, that which does not function.

Word Card 155

SELF-DEFEATING

When I embark upon an action which was previously unsuccessful I am backsliding. Figuratively, I have been to Waterloo before and I was defeated. Now I seek to return to the scene of my defeat. This is self-defeating.

• Defeats I encounter are usually traceable to me. *Judges* 11 is the story of Jephthah, a person who had a difficult time growing up because his mother had been a prostitute. As such he was not entitled to a share of his father's property. His brothers disowned him and he left Israel and moved to the land of Tov. There he formed a band of marauders and raided settlements. Later when the Ammonites began war against Israel, the Israelites sent for Jephthah and asked him to lead their army against the invaders. Jephthah, still smarting from the earlier insults and his expulsion, demanded that he be made the Chief of all Gilead if he were to fight and defeat the enemy.

The elders agreed and Jephthah and his band went into battle against the numerically superior forces of the Ammonites. Fearing a defeat, Jephthah swears a vow unto God, "If you deliver the Ammonites into my hand, then whatever comes through the door of my house to greet me when I return safely from the Ammonites, that shall be God's, and I will offer it as a burnt offering." Jephthah attacked and was successful. He crushed the enemy. When he returned home, his daughter, his only child, came out to meet him. She had her tambourine and was dancing. When he saw her he tore his clothes, knowing he would have to sacrifice the love of his life.

"My father, if you have sworn a vow, then do to me as you have sworn," his daughter said.

The card indicates the path of self-defeat. First, I must fear defeat. Then I must act out of the fear. Here Jephthah had made a vow out of fear that he would lose the battle. When I act out of fear as Jephthah did, I will come eventually to the point of self-defeat.

• Fear is an emotion and serves as a signal. To assimilate fear and to act out of fear will always be self-defeating.

• It is not enough to say that I am not addicted to drugs or alcohol. I am self-defeating when I load up on cholesterol-laden foods or when I overload on coffee or cigarettes. I no longer have respect for myself and my actions are self-defeating. I have forfeited my self-esteem.

Word Card 156

SHAME

Shame arises because of something which I have done or which someone with whom I identify has done. Shame is essential to my moral health because shame is a governor, like brakes on a car. Even though shame brings on self-reproach, it serves as a civilizing force. There is one caveat: I will never be ashamed of who I am or how I look or how I speak. I am who I am.

• Shame and disgust begin with fantasy. In the fantasy I am caught up in something generally seen as perverse. The other person's mere appearance is enough to trigger the sense of disgust or shame. Sometimes the fantasy involves the general public such as anyone at a dinner or anyone on public transportation. These perverse fantasies become alien bodies in my unconscious and are repressed by shame and disgust. When the time comes in life to form loving relationships with others, it becomes impossible because the fantasies now are directed towards the person or persons who are most worthy of my love. Shame and disgust are signals from the unconscious which need special attention. I look within for their origin.

• When I speak of a low down dirty shame, I am speaking about a situation about which everyone ought to be sorry.

• A crying shame portends a very unfortunate situation.

Word Card 157

SHARE

I am dealing with that which I have coming or with that which I must give to another. The prize will be cut into shares. My percent has to do with who I am and when I arrive on the scene.

A lion's share is all there is. If I am the leader, I will mete out to others first. If I come late, I do not demand a regular share.

• Being around people, even in a crowded environment, stimulates the person who likes to share. The Sacred Arts are Healing, Dream Interpretation, Oracular Use, and Story-telling. Each of these is a form of sharing. To share is a form of participation in the divine. When I share the solution to a problem or when I learn through trial and error, I am sharing, even though the sharing is sometimes with me alone.

Word Card 158

SHOULD

When I add the letters "er" to should I get the word shoulder. What I should do is what I must shoulder. I shoulder my responsibilities. I put my shoulder to the wheel. I stand shoulder to shoulder with my companion. I rub shoulders with the right people. I stay off the shoulder of the road. Everything I should do involves my shoulder.

• I should always consider the effect of my actions on others. Unless I become sensitive to the values of my family, friends, associates, and those with whom I work or do business, I am not shouldering my duty as a fellow human being. Everyone gains from being appreciated as a person. A kind and encouraging word will be remembered and treasured by the person who receives it. I will receive their good will. Everyone gains.

• When there is something I was prepared to do and did not but ought to have done, it becomes a case of woulda (would have), coulda (could have), shoulda (should have).

Word Card 159

SLAVE

To submit to another person and lose my personal freedom is to be a slave. This is the experience of an addict to food, drugs, alcohol, sex, or work. I am not in control of my life; I am a slave to it. I have become a bond servant.

• Some jobs are so tedious that the workers equate themselves to slaves. Production goes down as a result.

• Slavery is not exclusive to human activity. The process of creating slavery is in targeting a population and making slaves from members of that population. Slave-making is an archetypal activity which exists throughout all of Nature. Ants are prototypical slave-makers. There are species of ants which raid colonies of other species of ants and carry off their young. These they raise as slaves. The slaves become completely socialized members of the captor colony and never realize that their social behavior has been altered to suit their captors. The ant slaves work and exchange food with their captors just as if they had remained with their own species.

• The card requires an answer to the question of whether I am a parasite in my relationship with others. Or perhaps the opposite is true. Am I in a parasitic relationship in which I am the slave?

Word Card 160

STOP

When the bus arrives at my stop I get off the bus. When I press a string on a violin or push a button on a trumpet I create a stop. I press on a wound and I stop the bleeding. I am at an important juncture. When a law enforcer tells me to stop, I come to a halt. When my unconscious signals me to stop some activity in the outer world, my failure to do so will have consequences, sometimes in the form of an illness or an accident.

• Sometimes I need to stop and smell the roses; I need to relax from my daily routine.

Word Card 161

STRANGERS

Stranger symbolizes a universal human condition. After Adam and Eve were cast out of Eden, every person thereafter became a stranger to every other person and to themselves individually. When my love or my loyalty lies elsewhere, I am the stranger. If I see a tea-leaf floating in my cup or if my nose is itching, or if I see one moth flying towards another, strangers are coming. The arrival of strangers is unsettling and at the same time very exciting, especially if the stranger is tall and dark. The card alerts me to the approach of a stranger. When I reach the point in life where I can say, "I have never met a stranger," I will have crossed over to the transcendent.

• Two aspects of myself are at odds with each other. They are strangers to each other. Sometimes I am a saint. Sometimes I am a sinner. My expressions are always intense. I do not believe in half measures. I have tremendous energy and a willingness to work hard at being one thing or the other.

Word Card 162

STUPID

The difference between stupidity and ignorance is whether I have been exposed to this situation before. If I have never been exposed to it before, I am ignorant. If I have been in it before and have not learned how to deal with it, I am stupid. Stupid means that I am unwilling to learn from my mistakes. I relish the puerile and the foolish rather than the wise and the clever. I am ineffectual if I choose stupid over bright. A stupid life is senseless, inane, and pointless. *The Random House Webster's Unabridged Dictionary* lists over 200 nouns and adjectives as terms of reference meaning a stupid person or a stupid action; a few are horse's ass, birdbrain, cabbagehead, dumb bunny, lunkhead, mushhead, schnook, and woodenhead.

Word Card 163

SUCCESS

Success follows a series of failures. Success always comes about in the process of time and effort and because I have persevered in my efforts. Success, more than anything, is a decision not an accident. When I decide that I am on the road to success, the battle is over, for the battle was within me. When I realize that success is a decision, I no longer block my own progress.

• It is difficult to fathom, yet there is such a thing as fear of success. Success is so sought after and so desired that people who have it are the envy of others. Successful people are made into models for the rest of the world to emulate. Nevertheless, success does not always bring the satisfaction imagined. Underlying the fear of success is the fear of life itself. The source of such a fear is within the unconscious, in the inner self which is cutting me off from life by withdrawing from reality. Rather than recognize that it is internal, my usual response is to look outside of myself. If I say it is one of my parents, I incorrectly identify either my mother or my father as the one who is blocking me. It is neither of course. To love and live life fully and enjoy success as its byproduct happens by bringing together my unconscious and my conscious in a balanced harmony. Success often destroys its balance. I forget that I am just as dependent on the unconscious as I am on the conscious. True success is wholeness.

• Samson was a very successful person until Delilah robbed him of strength by cutting off his hair. It was the combination of his muscular body (consciousness) with the libido of his hair (the unconscious) which gave him his strength.

• At times I build my success by stepping over those who are closest to me. Oscar Wilde said it best, "It is not enough just to succeed; one's friends must also fail." Success is never comparing my home, bank balance, looks, or weight with others who have bigger homes, more money, better health, a cuter face, or a thinner body. Success is comparing what I have with someone who has less than I have. This leaves me satisfied and content.

Word Card 164

SUPPRESS

I want to keep something secret. I do not want my feelings to be exposed. When I take action against a person for some ill directed at me, I look first to quench the fire which is blazing within my being before I try to suppress it in someone else. I will talk it over first, I will be encouraged through discussion. I need to express before I suppress.

Word Card 165

TAKE

To take something which is not mine is not the same as taking something which is freely given. When I must surrender to adversity and the circumstances require me to take it like a man, I have to release my hostility realizing that there will be another day. What I undergo strengthens me. When I single out a person to be my sexual partner and determine to possess that person, I belong on a battlefield rather than in a courtship. I will let the person come to me. Everyone has to schlep once in a while. When it is my turn, I will take it and tote it. My take in life will be gravy when my work and efforts are honest.

• Which of these "takes" belongs to me? When it is time to take it easy, it means that my temperament is out of control. I am very angry. Or, I do not like to take a backseat to anyone. Or, I do not appreciate being the subordinate.

Or, I take care of business. Or, I take no prisoners.

Word Card 166

THREAT

The sword of Damocles hangs over his head by a single hair. When I threaten another, I am holding a sword over the other person's head. A threat is a promise of harm. For this reason it is dangerous to threaten. The other person will respond with violence. A threat which I make or a threat which I receive will put me in jeopardy.

Word Card 167

UGLY

"The Ugly Duckling" is a fairy tale about a newly hatched duck who was not well received by his sisters and the other barnyard animals because he was so ugly. They bit him, pecked away at him, and teased him. His life becomes one disaster after another. Even when a farmer tries to assist him, things go wrong. Eventually when he reaches adulthood he discovers his real identity: He is a swan and he is beautiful. The card reminds me that everything contains its opposite. What is ugly today has the capacity of beauty tomorrow.

Word Card 168

VICTIM

The early meaning of victim was that of a living creature who is put to death as a sacrifice to a deity. Today's sense of victim is my perception that I am being tortured or hurt by another. Rather, whatever suffering I am enduring had its genesis at my conception. No one is to blame for my persecution or oppression, not myself, not my parents and, amazingly, not even the perpetrator. It is quite difficult to conceptualize the fact that the person wielding the whip is not my victimizer. The process begins at conception and remains in place without addition or detraction of anything from who and what I am.

Word Card 169

VIOLATE

I violate my feminine when I neglect my spiritual side, when I fail to meditate, or when I live exclusively in my masculine side. Violation begins in the feminine and is executed in the masculine. These dual aspects of every human being have separate functions in every activity in the outer. The Adam and Eve myth is an example of how the process works. Eve initiates the process of disobedience. Adam executes it and eats the apple. Eve is cursed with labor pains. When the urge arises to erupt or to go berserk, it is the feminine within me that needs calming. When the urge is acti-vated, it is my masculine side which takes over and has to be brought under control.

Word Card 170

WAIT

Penelope was a celebrated princess of Greece who was married to Odysseus. During the absence of Odysseus, Penelope was approached by 108 suitors. She treated each one with disdain. Odysseus returned after 20 years and killed each of his 108 rivals. Homer wrote of Penelope's wait, calling her a model of feminine virtue and chastity.

• This means that I am contemplating making an unforeseen attack upon another. I am lying in wait. I am hiding my motives. I have taken up a concealed position where I wait. During this interval period, I must reconsider the plans I have made. Could it be that I have misjudged? The wait could be fortuitous. It is always better to bide my time before acting. When I reconsider, I can anticipate far fewer things which are likely to occur than those that probably will.

• When I ask someone to wait up it means that I am out of breath and racing to catch up with another.

Word Card 171

WEARY

To be weary is to be intensely fatigued. Weary carries a strong emotional emphasis. The body will lose its weariness after sleep. When I am weary because I am sick at heart I have great desire for the cessation of something and sleep will not help me.

Weary means that I am worn out. It may come because I am bored, because I may be jaded, or because I may be just plain disgusted. To refresh my mind and my spirit, I will energize my unconscious through meditation. I will put things into perspective. My weariness will be swallowed up by the new excitement.

WISE

Word Card 172

Being wise is being skilled in the hidden arts. It is in choosing my words carefully. It is learning the wizardry of the unconscious. When I learn discernment, putting aside as Paul said "the things of a child," I become both intuitive and judicious. My inner child is foolish and obtuse. When I move judgment out of the emotional chakra and into the heart chakra, wisdom will replace stubbornness and folly. Profundity can be permanently mine if I practice it.

• Wisdom is never thrust upon a person. I become wise by using logic, doing analysis, and remaining concerned with seeking objective truth. I become wise when I realize that everyone I meet is a potential teacher. I learn from the experiences of others as well as my own experiences.

• A wise person as opposed to a wise guy collects data and evaluates the information carefully before making determinations. A wise guy is someone who is an irrepressible smart aleck and knows it all. The wise guy is shrewd and street smart.

• The wise man is a person who is aware and knowledgeable. My task is knowing the difference between a wise guy and a wise man and deciding which I want to be.

WOMEN

Word Card 173

The female has caught the short end of the stick for over three millennia. When the rules of Judaism came into existence, there was an implicit rejection of the female presence in the Godhead. The First Commandment is an announcement that "I am the Lord thy God. Thou shalt have no other Gods before me." (*Exodus* 20:2,3). The "I" of the Speaker is a masculine figure. There is no mention of a female counterpart. Nor are other than male titles in Torah attached to this God. He is Lord and Master of all. Christianity continued the notion of male supremacy as did successor religions. The Koran continued this tradition by maintaining strict controls over women's rights and rejecting any god or goddess other than an imageless, male Deity. When Martin Luther founded Protestantism, one of his first proclamations was to outlaw devotion to Mary.

•This card has the sense of mistreatment at the hands of others. Prejudice against me because of who I am is a bitter pill to swallow. It is when I refuse to accept the imposition of labels which mark me as unequal that I am able to avoid the abuse others would heap upon me.

• Men often refer to their wives as the "old lady" or "little woman." Children sometimes call their mothers the "old lady." Such terms are disrespectful and are part of the demeaning process of women. The card suggests that I should examine my own speech patterns to determine whether I am putting down women.

• When a woman leaves a man or threatens separation, sometimes the man feels that his dominance is being challenged and becomes violent and abusive. A woman is a slave and does not have freedom or rights when she is in a relationship with a man who considers her his property.

• "Heaven has no rage, like love to hatred turned, nor Hell a fury like a woman scorned." William Congreve, who wrote this in 1697, might just as well have written the lines for today's men who stalk, attack, or otherwise abuse women after a break-up.

WONDERFUL

Word Card 174

• Imagination is the faculty which can fill me with wonder. Using my imagination, I can visualize a brilliant red rose and smell its sweet fragrance even though at the time I am peeling a pungent smelling red onion that is stinging my eyes and making them water. Or, as I walk down an alley at night, a branch on the ground may look to me like a snake, a shadow may loom as a person about to jump into my path or as a ghostly apparition. A falling leaf may be transformed into a fluttering butterfly. Whether my eyes are open or shut, the images of my imagination appear as if they are real and present. Wonder is within me and it is my imagination which brings forth within me a sense of wonder.

• Chaucer wrote of a nine-days' wonder in *Troilus and Criseyde*, something at which everyone marveled but which lasted only nine days. Today we call such an appearance a flash in the pan. That which appears as wonderful today may disappear tomorrow.

Word Card 175

WRONG

I am on a crooked course. I think I know the difference between what is right and what I am doing. I am mistaken. The last thing I want to do is to injure another. I must now consider whether my thinking could be erroneous, whether the relationship I am in might be unsuitable or even whether my conduct could in any way be considered unethical. That which is inappropriate does not suit me. What is improper is awkward. Denigrating another dishonors me. I will not answer slander with more slander. I should make what is wrong right.

• When I get up on the wrong side of the bed, my day is off kilter. Others see me as peevish. My foul mood affects everything I do.

• Being born on the wrong side of the tracks means that I come from an economically depressed area. Railroad tracks or expressways separate the poorer, industrial areas from the better neighborhoods. The card raises the possibility that I have created an artificial barrier which arbitrarily creates classes of uppers and lowers.

• When I encounter people who rub me the wrong way, it is critical that I do a self-examination to determine what it is about me which is being reflected in the others. If I point a finger at another, I am pointing four fingers at myself. That which affects my disturbance meter is describing an aspect of myself.

• It is a privilege to live in times when wrong is so prevalent. In times of strict dictatorships the ways of life are determined by the government. In times of democratic governments, repression is down. In such times, the challenge is to seek the balance between the wrong and the right.

• When someone gets me wrong, they have misunderstood where I am coming from. I need to clarify how I feel.

• When I bark up the wrong tree, I am like the dog who is helping the hunter who is after raccoons. The raccoon has run up one tree and the dog is barking up the wrong tree. Like the dog, I have been fooled.

Word Card 176

LOVE

In 1936, Edward VIII, king of the United Kingdom, abdicated the throne in order to marry Mrs. Wallis Simpson, a divorcée. In his abdication speech he said " . . . you must believe me when I tell you that I have found it impossible to carry the heavy burden of responsibility and to discharge my duties as king as I would wish to do without the help and support of the woman I love." He became the only British monarch to have resigned the Crown of his own free will.

The love which Edward felt for Wallis Simpson is a model for the world: Am I willing to surrender everything for my love of another?

• In *Troilus and Cressida*, Chaucer spoke of instantaneous romantic attraction, love at first sight. The concept is as ancient as humankind.

THE AUTHOR

Adam Bourgeois lives three blocks from where he was born in Chicago on Mother´s Day. Twenty-two years later he was practicing law and today he is still a trial practitioner. During some of the intervening years, he also served as a Cabinet officer under an Illinois governor and on the administrative staff of the mayor of Saint Louis. He administered several social programs around the United States during the Sixties. He also was a tenured Professor at The Ohio State University where he taught graduate and undergraduate students. He has lectured extensively. His adolescent years were spent in a Roman Catholic seminary. He has traveled a great deal, consulting other seekers and teachers along the way. He converted to Judaism twelve years ago, is married, and has three adult children. As a child he was bedridden for an extended period and to entertain him an aunt gave him a Ouija® Board and thus began his quest for the Philosopher´s Stone. His special project is writing about the idea of Pythagoras that everything is Number and a book on this subject will be available soon.

BIBLIOGRAPHY

Ammer, Christine. *American Heritage Dictionary of Idioms, The.* Boston New York: Houghton Mifflin Co., 1997

Arthur Rackham Fairy Book, The. Classics Illustrated with sixty-one color and black and white plates. New York: Weathervane Books, 1978

Barnhart, Robert K., ed. *The Barnhart Concise Dictionary of Etymology.* New York, NY: HarperCollinsPublishers, 1995.

Becker, Udo. *The Continuum Encyclopedia of Symbols.* Trans. Lance W. Garmer. New York: Continuum, 1994

Biedermann, Hans. *Dictionary of Symbolism.* Trans. James Hulbert. New York, New York: Facts on File, 1992

Brewer's Dictionary of Phrase & Fable. Revised by Adrian Room. New York, NY: HarperCollinsPublishers, 1995

Bruce-Mitford, Miranda. *The Illustrated Book of Signs & Symbols.* New York, New York: DK Publishing, Inc., 1996

C. G. Jung Letters. 2 vols. Selected and Edited by Gerhard Adler.Trans, R. F. C. Hull. Bollingen Series XCV. Princeton, New Jersey: Princeton University Press, 1953 (Vol .1) and 1973 (Vol. 2)

Campbell, Joseph with Bill Moyers. *The Power of Myth.* Ed. Betty Sue Flowers. New York: Anchor Books. A Division of Random House, Inc., 1991

Chapman, Robert L., Ph.D. with Barbara Ann Kipfer, Ph.D. *The Dictionary of American Slang.* Third Edition. Ed. Robert L. Chapman, Ph.D. New York: Harper Collins Publishers, 1998

Chetwynd, Tom. *A Dictionary of Symbols.* Vol. 2. Language of the Unconscious. Hammersmith, London: Thorsons. An Imprint of Harper Collins Publishers, 1982

Chetwynd, Tom. *How to Interpret Your Own Dreams. An Encyclopedic Dictionary.* New York: Bell Publishing Company, 1980

Chetwynd, Tom. *Dictionary for Dreamers.* Vol. 1. Language of the Unconscious. Hammersmith, London: Thorsons. An Imprint of Harper Collins Publlishers, 1972

Chevalier, Jean and Alain Gheerbrant. *A Dictionary of Symbols,* Trans. John Buchanan-Brown. Second Edition New York, New York: Penguin Books USA Inc., 1996

Cirlot, J. E. *A Dictionary of Symbols.* Trans. Jack Sage. Second Edition. London and Henley: Routkedge & Kega Paul, 1971

Collected Works of C.G. Jung, The. 20 vols. Trans. R. F. C. Hull. Editors: Sir Herbert Read, Michael Fordham, Gerhald Adler; Executive Editor: William Hull. Bollinger Series XX. Princeton, New Jersey: Princeton University Press

Conroy, Ellen. *The Symbolism of Color.* North Hollywood, California: New Castle Publishing Co., Inc., 1996

Cooper, J. C. *An Illustrated Encylopaedia of Traditional Symbols. With 210 Illustrations.* London: Thames and Hudson Ltd., 1979

Fontana, David. *The Secret Language of Dreams. A Visual Key to Dreams and Their Meanings.* San Francisco: Chronicle Books, 1994

Fontana, David. *The Secret Language of Symbols. A Visual Key to Symbols and Their Meanings.* San Francisco: Chronicle Books, 1994

Franz, Mary-Louise von. *On Divination and Synchronicity. The Psychology of Meaningful Chance.* Toronto, Canada: Inner City Books, 1980

Frutiger, Adrian. *Signs and Symbols. Their Design and Meaning.* Trans. Andrew Bluhm. New York: Watson-Guptill Publications, 1998

Graves, Robert. *Greek Myths. Illustrated Edition.* London: Penguin Books, 1984

Hamilton, Edith. *Mythology.* Illustrated by Steele Savage. First Black Bay Paperback Edition, 1998. Boston New York London: Little, Brown and Company, 1942

Hendrickson, Robert. *The Facts on File Encyclopedia of Word and Phrase Origins.* Revised and Expanded Edition. New York: Facts on File, Inc., 1997

Herder Dictionary of Symbols, The. Symbols from Art, Archaeology, Mythology, Literature, and Religion. Trans. Boris Matthews, Ph.D.. Eds. Deborah Farrell and Carole Presser. Wilmette, Illinois: Chiron Publications, 1993

I Ching or Book of Changes, The. The Richard Wilhelm Translation rendered into English by Cary F. Baynes. Foreword by C. G. Jung. Third Edition. Bollingen Series XIX. 1967: Princeton University Press, Princeton, New Jersey.

Jung, C. G. *Memories, Dreams, Reflections.* Recorded and Edited by Aneila Jaffé. Tranlated by Richard and Clara Winston. New York: Vintage Books, 1965

Lighter, J. E., Ed. *Random House Historical Dictionary of American Slang, Volume I And Volume 11.* New York: Random House, 1994, 1997.

Liungman, Carl G. *Dictionary of Symbols.* New York London: W. W. Norton & Company, 1994

Morris, William and Mary Morris. *Morris Dictionary of Word and Phrase Ori gins.* Second Edition. New York, NY: HarperCollinsPublishers, 1988

Owens, Lily, ed. *The Complete Brothers Grimm Fairy Tales. Illustrated.* New York: Gramercy Books, 1996

Owens, Lily, ed. *The Complete Hans Christian Andersen Fairy Tales. Illustrated.* New York: Gramercy Books, 1984

Shinn, Florence Scovel. *The Game of Life and How to Play It.* Marina del Ray, California: DeVorss & Company, 1925

Shlain, Leonard. *The Alphabet Versus the Goddess.* New York: Viking, 1998

Sideman, Belle Becker, ed. *The World's Best Fairy Tales.* 2 vols. Illustrated by Fritz Kredel. Pleasantville New York, Montreal: The Readers Digest Association, Inc., 1967

Stevens, Anthony. *Ariadne's Clue. A Guide to the Symbols of Humankind.* Princeton, New Jersey: Princeton University Press, 1999

Todeschi, Kevin J. *The Encyclopedia of Symbolism.* A Creative Breakthroughs Book. New York, New York: A Perigee Book, 1995

Torah. A Modern Commentary, The. Ed. W. Gunther Plaut. New York: Union of American Hebrew Congregations, 1981

Tresidder, Jack. *Dictionary of Symbols. An Illustrated Guide to Traditional Images, Icons, and Emblems.* San Francisco: Chronicle Books, 1998

Webber, Elizabeth and Mike Feinsilber. *Merriam-Webster's Dictionary of Illusions.* Springfield, Massachusetts: Merriam-Webster, Incorporated, 1999

Whiston, A.M., William, Trans. *Josephus. Complete Works.* Foreword by William Sanford LaSor, Ph.D, Th.D.Grand Rapids, Michigan: Kregel Publications, 1980

Zimmerman, J. E. *Dictionary of Classical Mythology.* New York Toronto London Sydney Auckland: Bantam Books, 1971

INDEX

D

E

F

G

L

M

N

O

P

Q

R

S

T

U

V

W

X

Y

Z